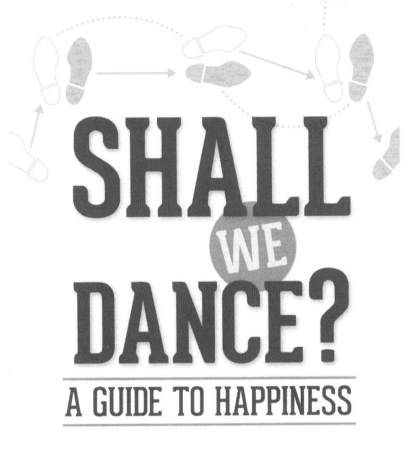

SHALL WE DANCE?

A GUIDE TO HAPPINESS

SHALL WE DANCE?

A GUIDE TO HAPPINESS

Erik S. Cooper, M.A., LMFT
and
Troy Wehmeyer

With Sharon Cooper and Jan Kraus

ERIK&TROY
PUBLISHING

Ogallala, NE

Cover design & illustrations by Drake Sauer
Author photo by: Drake Sauer
Editing and interior layout by Carla F. Blowey

ISBN: 978-0-692-20275-3

Library of Congress Control Number: 2014944455
Erik & Troy Publishing, Ogallala, NE

Printed in the United States of America

Published July, 2014

We dedicate this book to all those
who are seeking a safe place to be vulnerable;
who want to ask the questions that no one feels comfortable asking;
who need guidance, tools, friendship and connection
on their life's journey;
who desire to enrich their lives through their relationships;
and for those who
seek peace, contentment and satisfaction in their lives.

ACKNOWLEDGMENTS

"Gratitude is synonymous with thankfulness and appreciation. It is an attitude and acknowledgment of a benefit that one has received or will receive. Gratitude is not merely feeling grateful, but it is a choice to be motivated by that gratitude to do something outside of yourself. We extend our gratitude and appreciation to the following people who helped bring Shall We Dance into form." ~ ERIK & TROY

First, we want to thank Josie and Darrell with *Step By Step Dance Studio* in Las Vegas for the incredible experience we had learning to dance! Our experience with their dance studio is the inspiration for Chapters 3 and 4 of our book. Their understanding and mastery of dance instilled in us a passion to want to dance together! We hope our dance experience will inspire you to want to connect more with the people in your life! We also encourage you to consider Josie and Jim Lopez with Step By Step Dance Studio if you would like to re-connect with your loved one through dance. www.stepbysteplv.com

We are thankful for our friends at *Embassy Suites, Southeast Denver*, and *Royal Caribbean International, Mariner of the Seas*, for providing the perfect family atmosphere that inspired us to write this book! Healthy family relationships are emboldened at both of these locations. We thank them for helping us bring everyone closer to the happiness they are seeking.

We are thankful for Drake Sauer, our graphic artist, who created the incredible book cover and illustrations throughout the book. Drake's contribution with this project as an artist and as a son-in-law, has allowed him to design these illustrations with feeling and empathy for our readers. His amazing artistic and creative talent has enabled us to effectively convey our message with emotion and understanding.

We are grateful for our friend, Carla Blowey, and her enthusiastic participation as one of our editors. As an author and editor, her experience and editing skills were invaluable in helping us get this book published. We are grateful for her patience, creativity, organization, expertise and wisdom. We couldn't have done it without her. Please check out her website, www.dreamingkevin.com.

We thank Steve Warner, our friend and professional colleague, for his inspiration, humor and mentoring.

We are especially thankful for our wives, Jeni (Wehmeyer) and Leslie (Cooper), and our children, Bryce and Renee, Breezy and Drake, Emma and Olivia for their patience and support! We could not have completed our book without the encouragement, love and sacrifice that they so willingly provided us throughout this long process.

We also want to thank our fathers for their positive and loving influence in our lives. My father, Gary Wehmeyer, instilled in me (Troy) an empathy and a respect for others. Dad was my elementary and high school guidance counselor. As a father and as a counselor, Dad encouraged us to take a "walk in another person's shoes" before condemning or rejecting them. I (Erik) am grateful to my father, Steve Cooper, for instilling in me the courage, the ability and the belief that I can reach for something beyond my grasp and accomplish it. I appreciate his genuine belief in me that I can do anything I focus on.

We are deeply grateful to our mothers, Sharon Cooper and Jan Kraus, for the endless hours of their loving support throughout the writing of this book. Their contribution was invaluable on so many levels. First, as we shared our thoughts and philosophies with them, they helped us organize it into written form, and then edited the material – many times! Second, working together on this project with our mothers reinforced our connection to one another, and enriched our relationship within the family. This process has made us very aware of the importance and value of continuing to strengthen our relationships and reinforce the bond we have with all the members of our family.

Lastly, we are so grateful to God for the opportunity to connect with you through our book!

~ ERIK & TROY

CONTENTS

ABOUT ERIK & TROY

"SHALL WE DANCE? A Guide to Happiness
is a collaboration of counseling techniques, successful sales methods,
and life skills based on our experiences and insights." ~ **Erik & Troy**

Erik S. Cooper   I am a licensed Marriage and Family therapist in private practice. I have been providing therapeutic services to individuals and families for over 23 years in southwestern Colorado. I am also the Clinical Director of a 16-bed, male, adolescent residential treatment facility. I have been married to my wife and best friend, Leslie, for 23 years, and we have two beautiful teenage daughters, Emma and Olivia.

I started my career and life path working with at-risk boys and their families at a residential treatment facility in inner city Denver. It was there that I realized my passion for helping adolescents and their families discover character and the sacredness of relationships. It was also at this treatment center that I met my wife, Leslie.

In my 23 years of private practice, I have worked with thousands of clients and their families, individually and in groups. I have noticed that we all share a universal desire for happiness and a connection to others. I believe this desire is the golden thread that connects us to one another. Happiness and connection can only be found in the present. Thus, my ultimate goal as a therapist is to inspire people to be present at all times.

Our book is full of practical and user-friendly tools designed to help you stay focused on the present. Through our 30-year relationship, Troy and I have practiced these tools again and again and are now confident that it is time to share them with you. This is our passion…this is our calling.

Troy Wehmeyer I am a sales executive and commercial print distributor in western Nebraska. I have been married to my high school sweetheart, Jeni, for over 30 years. We have raised two happy children, Bryce and Breanne, who are now married and starting their own families.

I started my career and life path in my early twenties working for a large corporation in the insurance industry. I was part of the Regional Marketing Staff responsible for hiring, training and motivating agents. From there, I took a turn on the corporate path as I accepted a position as Sales/General Manager with a start-up down comforter/ textile manufacturer.

In my thirties, I chose to leave the corporate world and moved back home to Nebraska to be closer to extended family. I drew from all my sales experiences and started my own business as a commercial print distributor to large commercial accounts. The company has flourished and we service over 400 customers and generate over 1.1 million dollars in annual sales. My business is successful because it truly is a healthy family business. I have incorporated my wife, my children and my mother into the daily operations.

Throughout my 30 years in the sales industry, I have learned that people have one universal desire…a desire for happiness and a connection to others. I realized early on that whether it be a family member, a customer or a business deal, each of my interactions was an opportunity to connect with people and learn what makes them happy.

I have had thousands of interactions with people over the last thirty years and with Erik's help, I have developed tools and techniques that have made me a more successful sales person, husband, father and friend! We've practiced these tools with great success and it is now time to share them with you.

ERIK & TROY   What has made the project even stronger for us is that we invited our mothers, Sharon Cooper and Jan Kraus, to join us. While we focused on the concepts and the writing, Sharon and Jan helped us with organizing, transcribing, editing, and marketing. In the beginning, it was a challenge in finding time to get together to work on the book because half of us live in Nebraska, (Troy and Jan), the other half, (Erik and Sharon) live in Colorado. As the project evolved, each of us has settled into our respective roles. We have learned that flexibility, communication and compromise are essential to this process and that our individual perspectives must be honored and valued. We have realized throughout this five-year process just how important family truly is.

"When we unite, we can accomplish much more than we can alone. Joining forces can create a positive change and give us endless possibilities. Not only will we feel more connected to one another, but we will also feel stronger, more harmonious, and uplifted. Feeling a part of something greater than ourselves has been an experience that has enriched all of our lives."

~ Erik S. Cooper & Troy Wehmeyer

INTRODUCTION

"We Have Your Back"

Today, in our society, many people feel alone or disconnected to one another. Even if they don't admit it, many people feel helpless and powerless with regard to the direction of their lives and the quality of their relationships. They simply do not know what to do.

We wrote *Shall We Dance? A Guide to Happiness* because we believe sharing our personal and professional experiences could influence others to lead a healthy and successful life. We wrote this book as we were raising our children, nurturing our marriages, and working hard to provide for our families. During that time, we noticed that we weren't the only families trying to hold it all together! Our discussion began and we agreed that popular ideas, theories or tools for achieving a happy and successful life seemed to fade quickly in our changing and diverse culture.

We wished that when we were young men someone had taught us how to *apply* character strengths such as honesty, integrity and courage to our relationships. No one showed us the connection between choosing these character strengths and our self-confidence. Self-confidence is having the belief in ourselves that no matter what situation we encounter, we have the tools, resources and people in our lives to get us through anything. Having self-confidence will get us through our most challenging times and help us to live a happy life.

We are motivated by the idea that:
- Happiness is achievable for all of us.
- Happiness is determined more by our minds than by our circumstances.
- Happiness is the by-product of lifting others up.
- Happiness can only be experienced in the present.
- The principles in this book, when learned, practiced and mastered, will always have an outcome of happiness.

The quality of our life is contingent on the quality of our relationships – we need connections with each other. Ultimately, the quality of our happiness is dependent on the healthy connections we make with one another. We learned that we cannot do it alone. Over the years, and through many difficult challenges and transitions, we have declared, "I have your back," to demonstrate our love and support for one another.

"We have your back" is not just a catchy slogan but also a philosophy we live by every day.

"THE GOOSE STORY"
A Lesson in Relationships

"Next fall, when you see Geese heading south for the winter, flying along in a 'V' formation, you might consider what science has discovered as to why they fly that way: as each bird flaps its wings, it creates an uplift for the bird immediately following. By flying in 'V' formation the whole flock adds at least 71% greater flying range than if each bird flew on its own.

People who share a common direction and sense of community can get where they are going more quickly and easily because they are traveling on the thrust of one another.

When a goose falls out of formation, it suddenly feels the drag and resistance of trying to go it alone and quickly gets back into formation to take advantage of the lifting power of the bird in front. If we have as much sense as a goose, we will stay in formation with those who are headed the same way we are.

When the Head Goose gets tired, it rotates back in the wing and another goose flies point. It is sensible to take turns doing demanding jobs with people or with geese flying south.

Geese honk from behind to encourage those up front to keep up their speed. What do we say when we honk from behind?

Finally, and this is important, when a goose gets sick, or is wounded by gunshots and falls out of formation, two other geese fall out with that goose and follow it down to lend help and protection. They stay with the fallen goose until it is able to fly, or until it dies. Only then do they launch out on their own, or with another formation to catch up with their group. If we have the sense of a goose, we will stand by each other like that."

WE INVITE YOU TO JOIN US IN OUR JOURNEY TOWARD HAPPINESS!

Our book, *Shall We Dance? A Guide to Happiness* is a blue print for achieving peace, contentment and satisfaction for yourself and the people around you. The ideas and principles we present to you have been tested and applied over the past 30 years in our professions (as a marriage and family therapist and as a salesman) and in our personal lives. These principles work all of the time, with everyone in our lives.

We wrote this book to create a resource and a culture to support, influence and inspire one another.

We have your back!

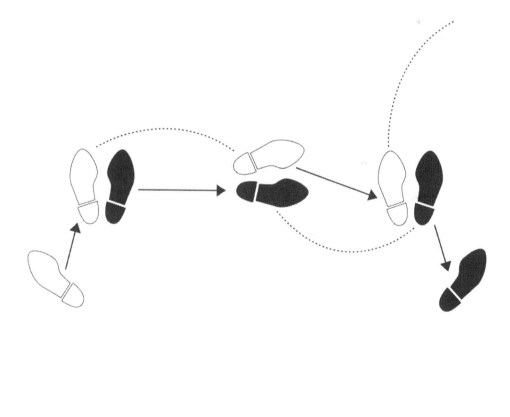

Part I

ARE YOU THRIVING OR JUST SURVIVING?

Do you find yourself avoiding friends and relatives…even your spouse? Are you skittish when the phone rings? Do you worry it is another request from friends and family to get together? Do you cringe at the thought that someone wants something from you?

Is it an unwritten rule in your house that when the phone rings, you screech, "Who is it? Who is it!?" and you follow with, "Don't answer it! Let them leave a message!" Is that the way things having been working in your house lately?

Have you begun to isolate yourself from everyone in your personal life…feeling as though this is the only way to get through each day? Do you sometimes feel the need to insulate yourself against the world?

Surprisingly, with these feelings driving your world, you are still meeting the demands of your job…well, sort of? You're getting by…at least until tomorrow. Perhaps, you are stronger than you think. You may be more resilient and more resourceful than you realize.

Have you wondered if there is *more* to you?

WHO'S AT THE HELM?

Who is driving your life? Many of us make decisions by what we are feeling at that moment. Whether that feeling is joy, fear, sadness or anger, crises and chaos are inevitable. Why? Emotions are inconsistent and unpredictable. That is why decisions, based solely on emotion, cannot help but be inconsistent and unpredictable. If you are feeling angry due to what has transpired that day, decisions you make in that moment are more than likely to be based out of that anger. What makes you angry on Monday may not have the same effect on you on Friday.

Do you want your decisions to come from a place that is such a variable – your emotions? Do you want to allow your emotions to be in the driver's seat steering your life, making your life unpredictable and inconsistent?

Our intention is to help you achieve a degree of peacefulness, contentment and satisfaction each day. This is what we call "happiness." We will give you what you need – namely, the tools to successfully navigate through life's obstacles by becoming aware of the value and the power of your intentions, motivation and focus.

THE BLADE IN THE WIND

Picture a field of grass. What does it look like when it is healthy and thriving?

The field at its healthiest appears to be and is strong, flourishing, flexible and pliable. In a thriving field, the grass is green, blowing in the wind; rich in how the flexible blades move, adaptable to changes in weather. The healthy blades of grass are strong, bending to the dictates of breezes, wind, storms. The field can overcome challenges from environmental elements. The field thrives.

However, when this same field is at its unhealthiest, it is rigid, fragile and abrasive. The once-thriving blades of grass are stiff. The field may weather some challenges brought on by nature but unlike the thriving field, this field does not do as well as it did when it was green and healthy.

Merely surviving is not the goal here – not for the field of grass nor for you. Instead, *thriving is the goal.*

Similar to fields of green, humans also need to strive for thriving instead of just surviving. Why? You cannot build a healthy marriage or create nourishing relationships that have longevity based upon the goal of just surviving. The goal of thriving gives us what we need to be able to achieve peace, contentment and satisfaction in our lives.

SURVIVING OR THRIVING?

All of us know at least one person who goes through life experiencing drama after drama, crisis after crisis. These same folks make their decisions based solely upon their emotions. They tend to put their feelings in the driver's seat of their life experiences. Consequently, they soon discover that their lives are filled with more crisis and chaos than they want or can manage. In order to function, they are forced to think of all the "what ifs" in life because they are operating in a *reactive mode* which is a very stressful existence. This kind of reactive action is what we call *surviving*. Just getting by.

However, when we choose not to allow emotions to rule our lives, we are able to operate in a more *responsive* or *proactive* manner. In this way, we can achieve consistency and predictability in our lives, and it is easier to push through the many day-to-day challenges that are sure to face us.

An important fact of being *proactive* instead of reactive is that we can operate more from a place of character as part of our inner-being and decision-making process.

Being proactive allows us to thrive and not merely survive.

It is important for you to remember that you have a choice as to which mode you use to live your life. You can choose to be reactive or proactive. It's up to you.

Do you want to merely survive or do want to weather life's storms like the strong, pliable blades of grass and thrive?

You cannot *not* make a choice! It is one way or the other. Which is it for you? Which do *you* choose?

HOW DO YOU MAKE YOUR DECISIONS?

When we are making our decisions based upon how we feel in that particular moment, we are essentially in survival mode. Life is unpredictable and inconsistent. On the other hand, when we make decisions based on our character strengths and not our intellect, we are operating from a predictable and consistent place. When we operate from a predictable and consistent place, we can always count on the outcome of contentment and peace.

Learning to make decisions from a centered, consistent and fixed place can influence how we interact with others. This process is vital as it effects how we think, feel, perceive and present ourselves.

We urge you to resist using your emotions to influence and drive your decision-making process. You can still be aware of your emotions. However, we passionately suggest that you not use this as the sole compass for your decision-making. You are less likely to feel hijacked by your emotions when you are able to identify and understand what you are feeling.

This is the centerpiece of our book, *Shall We Dance,* and we promise it can be life changing for you. Whether you are worried about your family, your romantic relationships, business or social contacts –whatever is at the front of your thoughts right now – we can teach you how to change your focus. Change your focus and you change your belief. Change your *belief* and you change your *life*.

Our goal is to help you identify and cultivate an awareness of having the power to choose where you want to place your focus.

JUGGLING LIFE

Balancing relationships at work and home creates many challenges. The workplace can demand so much of our energy and focus that we are drained when we get home. With little energy left, we are unable to give our family the attention that they need and deserve.

While it is necessary to hold a job so that we have a steady means of providing financial resources for our families, it is equally important to maintain family relationships which feed our needs and bring happiness.

DO YOU HAVE TIME?

We began working on this book in 2010, when according to the U.S. Department of Labor, unemployment hovered around 10%, with fluctuations even higher throughout the country.[1] Our motivation to help was to awaken the happiness quotient within. Then the need accelerated with so many people being out of work, and even more people worried about being laid off or fired. It is hard to raise the level of feeling good about our lives when life is in transition.

It touched our lives as well, sometimes too closely. Our brothers, sisters and neighbors either lost their jobs or were about to be laid off. For some, a sense of work security was snuffed out when the jobs people held for years were eliminated. Further, those suddenly jobless individuals were finding their lives turned upside down – forced to change careers or find work they never imagined doing, barely able to make ends meet. Some were laid off, while others were fired or their jobs eliminated. Fewer jobs were listed and companies deliberately stopped growing. The workplace, as we have known it, forced some people who were unprepared for this kind of change into life-changing decisions.

However a career or job ends, the resulting emotional letdown feels like an open wound that never heals. There is no time clock for emotionally getting over being fired or laid off from work. The feeling of being let go can live on, and get in the way of living life. It is not unusual for marriages to be destroyed. Many times, the children in the family who try to survive these life traumas become silent victims. Often these children assume the role of a parent, trying to take care of a depressed family member.

It is often said that landing a job is an easier task when you already have one. It is next to impossible to try to "sell yourself" in a competitive marketplace when you are feeling let down about no longer being needed at your former job. Feeling like a non-entity at a workplace that functions without you can be a real ego-scraper.

Foreclosures and bankruptcies continued at all-time record highs. Consider this, those who still had a job to go to were grateful just to *have* a job, in spite

---

[1] Bureau of Labor Statistics, U.S. Department of Labor, THE EDITOR'S DESK, Unemployment in December 2010 on the Internet at **http://www.bls.gov/opub/ted/2011/ted_20110111.htm** (visited MARCH 01, 2013)

of the fact that many people did not like what they did for a living. *Like* is a word that does not enter into the picture when *need* is the priority.

In this work climate, it was not unusual to hear someone say, "I have to work harder than ever before so I don't lose my job. My boss treats me badly because he knows I can't leave. I need to watch my step at work. There are people out there who actually want my job." According to a 2010 CNNMoney.com report by staff reporter, Julianne Pepitone, "Fewer than half of U.S. workers are satisfied with their jobs, the lowest level since record-keeping began 22 years ago…The Conference Board's survey polled 5,000 households, and found that only 45% were satisfied in their jobs."[2]

We are sure that same poll would still be valid today and the results would either hold or be greater. That amounts to the fact that there are many "unhappy" workers out there. Moreover, this is the reason why customer service is at an all-time low. It is difficult to give service when you are not satisfied with your job. It is not impossible, but not likely either.

MEETING THE DAILY GRIND

It is not hard to understand why meeting the demands of daily life in our relationships with spouses, children, friends and associates becomes more difficult by the moment when stress is a factor. It is clear why so many of us choose to limit volunteering time and service to our community. It is also understandable why so many of us feel "it's all about me" and choose not to step "outside of ourselves" and reach out to others.

People become selfish when they feel they are not getting what they need. They struggle to hold onto what they have and are unwilling to share with others or give of themselves. Holding onto things and collections makes for a numb existence.

HOW DO YOU FEEL?

Do you ask yourself, "Is this all there is in life?" Do you feel sad, lonely, angry or simply not good enough? If you do, please know that you are not alone. It is not uncommon for people to experience dissatisfaction and discontentment.

---

[2] Pepitone, Julianne. "U.S. job satisfaction hits 22-year low." CNN.COM, 5 January 2010. Web. 1 March 2013. **www.money.cnn.com/2010/01/05/news/economy/**

FACE FORWARD, NOT BACKWARD

Generally, people have more self-awareness than they think they do. After years of providing individual and family counseling, Erik knows that the majority of those seeking help are able to identify specific factors causing problems in their lives when asked the right questions. They know what they are tired of; they know what sickens them; and they know what bothers them about their spouses, their bosses and other elements of their lives.

Early in the therapy process, Erik will say to a client, "If you were running a race, our first challenge would be to turn you around so that you can focus on the finish line. Staying focused on the past (facing backward) will keep you thinking, feeling and perceiving as you did in the past – only surviving the race to get to the finish line. On the other hand, looking forward will give you something to reach for – your goal of thriving beyond the finish line. You run a much stronger and faster race when you are facing forward versus running the race facing backwards.

Merely surviving is not the goal here. Instead, *thriving is the goal.*

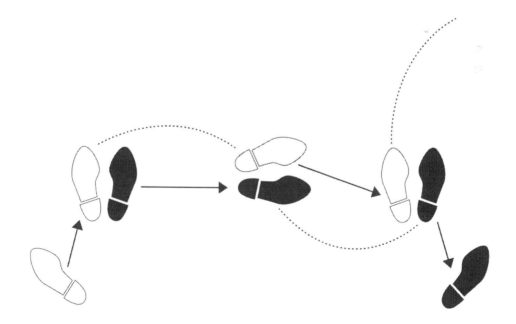

SHIFTING YOUR FOCUS
Discovering the Power of Choice

Simply put, we want you to change your focus. You choose where you want to place your focus. We know that what you focus on and where you place your attention, will set the target of what you will reach. If you focus on something that you would rather not have happen, then, that is where your attention will be – on the negative – exactly on what you don't want.

For example, let's say we showed you a shiny red apple and said, "Don't focus on that shiny red apple." What do you think is likely to happen? Right. You will not be able to stop thinking about that shiny red apple. You can see it, smell it and you can almost taste it.

The only way to stop thinking about that shiny red apple is to focus on something else, perhaps a fuzzy orange peach. We are suggesting a technique that is applicable now so that you can see change happen immediately.

Change your focus...change your life. Instead of concentrating on the things in your life that you are sick and tired of and all the obstacles that stand in your way and keep you from getting what you want, you need to turn around. Remember that half the battle of starting to make changes is to run your "race" while facing forward, not backward.

A LITTLE "HITCH" IN YOUR GET-A-LONG. IT'S ONLY TEMPORARY.

Chances are this technique is new to you. We do not expect you to turn your focus around without a hitch. Remember, you are not alone in learning to redirect your focus.

We can help you learn how to focus on what you *do* want, as well as how to keep what you *don't* want off your radar. You will soon feel confident that you are placing your energies where you want them to be, and consequently, refocusing your life. It is a *relearning process* where we'll help you match up your behaviors with methods and tools, allowing you to shift your response and focus on what really serves you.

Imagine a houseplant that needs light in order to survive and grow. Whatever part of that plant receives the most light is the part that grows the most. The parts that do not receive light will soon become lifeless. When light is refocused on the plant, it suddenly has what it needs to become green, healthy and strong, full of life again!

What or where do you shine the most light on in your life? Are you shining light on relationships or are you shining light on "keeping up with the Jones'?" When you shift your focus, you will be able to figure out why certain parts of your life may have gone from being full of life to lifeless. By shifting your focus, you can revive your relationships; similar to reviving parts of the plant.

HERE IS YOUR CHALLENGE

Begin looking at your life from four different perspectives: mental, emotional, physical and spiritual. Each of these four perspectives are components of the whole self. Each of the four perspectives may differ in size but together they complete the whole.

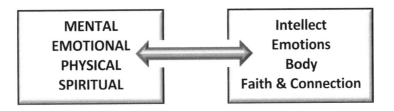

MENTAL	Intellect
EMOTIONAL	Emotions
PHYSICAL	Body
SPIRITUAL	Faith & Connection

You are about to discover the composite that most resembles you. This composite will give you additional insights about the people who are important to you. You will learn why these people matter to you. You will have a deeper understanding of why people behave the way they do and why you react to certain behaviors as you do.

Imagine that all four perspectives combine to make up an entire circle. In the middle of that circle is the core, the "real you."

As you begin to make changes in each of the four perspectives, you will find that your perception of the situations and people around you will change. That is exactly the pivot point when things in your life will begin to change for you. It is a new happening and a new start.

THE FOUR PERSPECTIVES

- MENTAL -

The *mental perspective* represents your intellectual self. Intellect knows no emotion. It can't. It is logical. Can you mentally redirect your thoughts? Can you treat your mental abilities as if they were a muscle? Are you able to exercise that muscle and make it stronger? The answer is yes.

If your tendency is to look at the negative side of things, are you able to train yourself to switch from thinking negatively to thinking positively? What if you discover that your mental ability is like a muscle? It is! The more you exercise that "mental" muscle, the stronger it becomes, and you can change the source of your thought.

When you exercise the "mental" muscle, you will begin to look at the positive side of things rather than focusing on the negative. It's like waking up from a long nap. You wake up feeling refreshed and focused. In this case, when you switch from negative to positive, you wake up believing in yourself – believing that your day will go well. "Maybe my spouse is not as terrible as I thought," or "Maybe there are some personality traits that I actually like about my spouse."

- EMOTIONAL -

The *emotional perspective* represents your emotional self. It knows no logic. All it knows is emotion. Emotions can be both real and not so real. Emotions are a part of everything that happens to you. It is important to feel –to be aware of and notice your emotions. It is critical to let yourself have emotions without judgment.

While it is important to honor your emotions, it is not so good to make decisions based solely on how you are feeling at that moment– especially when making decisions that require some logic. We all can relate to this and probably even know a few people who rely solely on emotions for their decision-making. When this happens, we know that those decisions tend to be inconsistent and unpredictable.

The emotional perspective drives your emotional intelligence and represents your ability to recognize and identify with how you are feeling at any given time. The emotional component is an important regulator. How are you motivated by your emotions? How do you want to be motivated by your emotions? How do you want to motivate yourself using the information provided by your emotional perspective?

The emotional perspective offers you the ability to self-regulate. It is how self-control is formed and it is how we learn to live with other people. The emotional perspective provides us with the ability to read social cues from those around us. Emotional perspective gives us the ability to connect with others. How we connect with others is how we build and keep relationships.

Sometimes when people get hurt emotionally, they shut themselves off from their emotional perspective, precipitated by having had a relationship or two go wrong. If you have ever been hurt in a love relationship, you might have promised yourself this hurt will "never happen again." This is one promise that is next to impossible to keep.

It is normal to react to pain by wanting to protect our feelings. We don't want to suffer hurt. It is painful. It is uncomfortable. As the result of a love relationship gone sour, you probably did not want to open your heart again to those feelings that might bring back that kind of hurt.

We understand. However, we can tell you that unless you do open yourself up emotionally, you won't be able to connect with anyone else on an emotional level. That emptiness is sure to leave you sad and empty.

~ PHYSICAL ~

The *physical perspective* is about self-discipline and being focused on your body – your physical being. For example, consider the amount of energy it takes for you to get off the couch, especially when you don't want to get off the couch but know you should! Self-discipline comes into play when people move forward in spite of what they're feeling. As much as we need to monitor our mental and emotional outlook, we also need to exercise our bodies for physical well-being. Take care of your body. It is the house in which you live. You only get one house. It is really about the choices you make in the present. Success is achieved when you are able to focus on and exercise each level, giving your life more balance.

People have a tendency to live out their lives in pretty much the same way they treat their bodies. Do you know people who are hard on their bodies? Do you know someone who doesn't get enough rest, consumes too much alcohol or takes medications that are not prescribed? Or someone who overeats and lives a sedentary life and takes too many risks? In addition, let's consider the "weekend warriors" who wait until the weekend to spend hours at the gym over-exercising and torturing their bodies.

It's not surprising that we tend to treat our relationships in the same manner that we treat our bodies.

PROACTIVE BEHAVIORS VS. TAKING MEDICATION

If you are motivated to begin a health plan to improve your physical well-being, it is helpful to understand a hormone called, "serotonin." Serotonin levels affect mood. Symptoms of depression are known to be associated with lower levels of serotonin. Exercise and good nutrition will boost your serotonin levels.

Research shows exercising for 30-45 minutes daily will increase your serotonin levels. When patients use antidepressants, they are essentially helping their bodies build up levels of serotonin with chemicals. Exercise is one of the natural, pro-active methods of increasing serotonin.

Here is an example to consider. Let's say someone is mildly depressed due to certain life situations. A therapist might suggest that, before trying medication to treat the depression, the patient could begin working on changing thoughts and behaviors, as well as adding a balanced diet and exercise. People tend to feel better, look better and often take better care of themselves by adjusting their body chemistry through increased activity. All of these changes work to impact self-esteem in a positive way. Adding exercise and activity to their routines improves relationships and changes belief systems.

˗ SPIRITUAL ˗

Spirituality is the dynamic web that connects us to God or a higher power as well as to one another. It creates a common bond comprised of compassion, empathy, forgiveness, gratitude, generosity, concern for others and love.

Spirituality includes a personal search for meaning in our life. It impacts how we relate to others and ourselves. Spirituality enhances the development of our character strengths.

We believe that staying aware of your spirituality will enhance your quality of life. Your personal concept of spirituality may change with your age and life experiences, but it always forms the basis of your well-being, helps you cope with stressors large and small, and affirms your purpose in life.

We believe *The Peace Prayer of St. Francis* supports the concepts shared in this book. We hope it will provide as much comfort to you as it does for us.

THE PEACE PRAYER
of ST. FRANCIS

Lord, make me an instrument
of your peace.
Where there is hatred, let me sow love;
Where there is injury, pardon;
Where there is doubt, faith;
Where there is despair, hope;
Where there is darkness, light;
And where there is sadness, Joy.

O Divine Master,
Grant that I may not so much seek
to be consoled as to console;
To be understood, as to understand;
To be loved, as to love;
For it is in giving that we receive,
It is in pardoning that we are pardoned,
And it is in dying,
that we are born to eternal life.

RELATIONSHIPS ARE DANCES

Relationships are like dances. Dancing is a give and take motion where partners mutually respond to one another as they move in unison to the beat of the music. Using dance as an analogy allows you to visualize yourself dancing with the people in your life in unison to the rhythm of life's music.

DIFFERENT DANCES FOR DIFFERENT RELATIONSHIPS

Let's suppose you choose to change *how* you are dancing in your relationships. Perhaps those relationships don't feel right, you feel misunderstood, taken advantage of or you just have the sense that things aren't right. Suppose a few of those relationships such as your spouse, your children or your boss are critically important to you. It might seem as though there has been no one to help you understand why things are falling a little short of your desires. Trust us. *Now* you have help and *you can change* your dance!

We can promise you this: when you use our concept of "relationships are like dances", you will have the tools to identify all your relationships from a different viewpoint. Each relationship creates its own dance and varies in its depth, emotion and importance but the dance steps remain the same. When you focus on the interaction of the dance, you can be "present" to what is happening now – in this moment – with your thoughts and actions. Our job is to teach you how to stay focused on the present.

When you recognize a relationship as a dance, you become more aware of the actions and reactions within the relationship that create an undesirable outcome. When you are more aware of those actions and reactions, you will be better equipped and more skilled to make the changes necessary to achieve positive and healthier interactions! Together, you and your partner can create a "new" dance that can transform your relationship. We hope that once you begin seeing your relationships as dances, you will integrate this tool in your thinking process and it will become a skill that you can use for the rest of your life.

A VIEW OF THE AUTHORS' CREATIVE WRITING PROCESS

Coming up with the idea for the book was easy! However, organizing and compiling the chapters was the hardest part, so Troy and Erik decided to "rev up" their creative process. It happened that Troy and his wife, Jeni, planned to take a vacation in Las Vegas, where they would have an opportunity to take dance lessons.

Troy and Erik had an "a-ha" moment when they both realized that the dance lessons might be an opportunity to illustrate their concept of how relationships are like a dance.

As a marriage and family therapist, Erik wanted to capture the intimate disclosures that Jeni and Troy were willing to reveal. Erik knew that by documenting what the two became aware of during their weeklong dance experience, the couple's discoveries would be very insightful for them.

Throughout the years of their friendship, Erik knew that his brother-in-law had an issue with dancing in general, and Erik surmised that Troy was feeling conflicted about the upcoming dance lessons. Troy had mixed emotions about the dance lessons because he had never felt comfortable on the dance floor. In fact, Troy could not remember the last time he and Jeni had danced!

On one hand, Troy was excited to travel to Las Vegas with Jeni, feeling this time together would be a renewal of the relationship they had enjoyed since high school. Jeni was certainly up for the idea and looked forward to special "us time" with Troy. Jeni also agreed the trip could have a dual purpose – time with Troy as well as research for the book. However, neither Troy nor Jeni ever imagined that their experiences would prove to be "life-changing" for both of them.

TAKING NOTES

Erik knew that journal writing was a successful counseling technique, and that Troy and Jeni could apply this method to record their experience in Vegas. Erik asked that each keep a separate journal and avoid sharing their respective entries until they returned from their trip. By keeping their entries separate, neither Troy nor Jeni could influence what the other wrote, making their observations even more revealing. Erik planned to add his clinical observations when they returned and the three of them could discuss the journal entries together.

Throughout the chapter, you'll see Erik's thoughts and therapeutic point of view inserted between Troy and Jeni's comments, offering insights into the deeper meaning of the couple's emotions and the "a-ha" moments they experienced.

What Troy and Jeni learned might surprise you. Their new personal awareness will probably apply to you more than you expect. And, it may be just what you need to rebuild your own relationships or to create new ones. Yes, relationships are the key. Let's continue on to see how Troy and Jeni used their dance lessons to reconnect with one another.

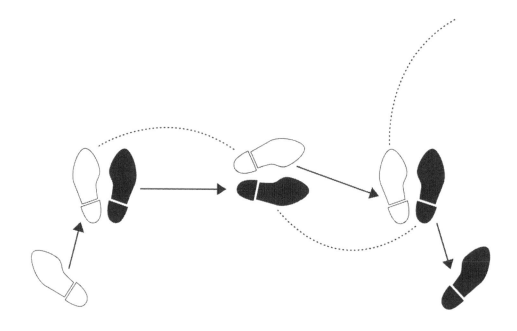

TROY AND JENI'S JOURNAL

DAY ONE: "Two left feet. Can we really do this?!"

TROY: "I'm surprised at the way the dance instructor, Darrell, moved from couple to couple, introducing himself and trying to put people at ease – kind of like a dance in itself. For our first activity, the instructor asked each couple to face one another and take a minute to look into each other's eyes. It's funny how uncomfortable people can become when looking at someone they've known for a number of years.

My thoughts were about how uncomfortable I felt on the dance floor. It feels like a "chink" in my "strong man armor" – that invisible wall guys set up when we're unsure of ourselves. I find it funny that I feel unsure. After all, this is *Jeni*...my wife of many years!

I looked into Jeni's eyes and wondered what she was thinking. Later, Jeni told me that she felt uncomfortable too, and a little powerless, not knowing what to expect. She worried about being able to learn the dance steps. But, when we did look into each other's eyes, we saw a best friend.

We had just finished the first two-hour dance session when I had my first big "aha" moment. Today, my learning point is that as the man, I need to have more confidence...more belief in myself. I also learned that I needed to connect more frequently with my wife. You might think that after all these years together and with two nearly grown children, we already do that – connect with one another. But, much to my surprise, I had not noticed her much lately and the lately kept getting later.

I also learned that when I actively lead Jeni, she responds to my lead but only if we are in tune with one another and are focusing on each other.

It's up to me to anticipate the next move that's coming, from a change in the music to a change in the dance steps. In that way, I can prepare her for the next move before it happens, so she can follow my intentions. My body language provides cues to her, allowing her to pick up on my next move. All in all, it works well if we focus on one another. I'm learning that men have short attention spans and women have long memories.

After just one day, I learned that dancing gives me extra confidence. I feel that I have a little more self-esteem now than I had yesterday before I had taken any lessons. Now, I find I am looking forward to tomorrow, anticipating that I will be even better, because I now understand how connecting with one's partner can actually temper the quality of the dance. My reaction is not a "stretch." I feel that my new self-assuredness on the dance floor is adaptable to our daily lives. I wonder how my new awareness will spill over into my other behaviors with Jeni. We'll see.

Today, I sense that Jeni and I have a better grasp on our relationship and can deal with whatever comes our way in the future. I'm not just talking about dance lessons here. I trust that we'll be stronger as a couple and better able to handle what comes our way because we have learned to connect with one another…working as a team. Today's positive experience has reminded us that we are not alone. Jeni and I are fortunate. We have each other. An interesting thought – this is the kind of intimacy that differs from sexual intimacy. This is the forever kind of thing. This is the new me now. On that note, I can't help but wonder what Jeni is thinking. Wish I could peek at her notes."

JENI: "It is just day one. My thoughts today include how comfortable I feel now in comparison to yesterday. I am excited that Troy and I are figuring this out together. Before we came here, I wasn't so sure. I was worried that, somehow, we might not be in sync with the instructor. There was a lot that we needed to figure out. I thought about the fact that part of our learning will take place with strangers. I feel better that all of us will be starting out with the basic steps.

Here is an interesting piece we learned. The instructor taught us something he calls a "home base move" which is foundational. This is a step or a position that we can opt to go back to when we get mixed up. "Home base" enables us to start again. We can rebuild our next moves from there. It's like a second chance or an "erase button" used to remove the scrambled moves and restart from there. Everything that we are learning can improve from this home base move. We can practice turns and other moves with our foundation remaining the same.

When a house is built, it is likely to last if the foundation is strong. If we misstep on the dance floor, we are able to begin again. Home base is our restart, our do-over place. We choose, as a couple, to begin again. We support each other's needs. Home base – I like that.

What I also find interesting is that the instructor will be teaching more than one routine. He will show us a group of moves that ultimately will be put together to form a dance routine. While Troy and I will be learning to dance as a couple, we will also have opportunities to dance with others, so that we can sample different dancing styles. In this way, we can see how we adapt to others and how others adapt to us. People lead and follow in different ways.

Now, I am starting to feel more comfortable because I think we can do this. Before we arrived in Las Vegas, I wasn't so sure how this idea would turn out for us. Now, I am a believer. We can do this. I'm beginning to feel good about this experience and I am feeling better about us."

ERIK: *Troy felt more energy when he focused on Jeni. When Jeni focused on him, he felt great, more connected. Connection happens when we focus on the moment. It is intimacy on several levels. When connectedness is incorporated into any relationship, dancers become better dancers and life partners become better partners, both on and off the dance floor.*

Jeni points out the importance of using "home base" as an emotionally safe place to start over. Home base is an agreement we make with each other to start over and reset when our dance/relationship is out of sync. Just as Troy and Jeni used home base to start over when their dance steps were out of sync, you, too, can use this same concept to start over when your relationships are out of synch.

When home base does not exist, our arguments, disagreements and issues often escalate and go unresolved.

DAY TWO: We got this! Or not…?!!

TROY: "Today, I saw how much the man is involved within the framework of a dance relationship (as the man is with life relationships). I understand just how much a spouse or partner counts on the other person to be a guide through a dance experience. Knowing this gave me a good feeling, making me see that my role is important to the dance. I admit I enjoy taking the lead.

Guys, take heed. If a man has little or no self-confidence, his partner knows it. This is true in dancing and in life. The result is that a lack of self-confidence on either side throws everything off. Much to my surprise, a dance relationship is a delicate balance. I find I am surprised at how easily that delicate balance can be taken down by a lack of confidence.

You can be so afraid of trying that you never get started. The key for Jeni and me was that we signed up for the dance lessons, putting ourselves in a position that we had to do it. We made a commitment, both personally and financially. This commitment pushed us into keeping our word with each other. We are in this together. At this point, I am glad we took the risk.

I will admit that I was, and still am, a little uncomfortable. My ego causes me to feel fear and separation. But by putting myself in a situation that has some emotional risk, I am bound to draw from it and grow on a personal level. I find that it's hard for me to grow without some discomfort or emotional pain.

The other side of the coin is that this experience solidifies how important it is to find fun in everything we do together. By taking a few risks and choosing to be vulnerable with one another, or even playful, we can create a new light and warmth in our relationship."

JENI: "We've just returned to our hotel room from our second dance lesson. We learned more dance steps today and I feel good about our performance on the dance floor. More important, Troy and I are enjoying each other. That makes me feel good. I can see that as a couple our confidence level is higher. We're even starting to feel that we can become better dancers than we had thought possible."

ERIK: *It's possible to be so caught up in the demands of life that we forget how to be in a relationship. Thinking in dance terms, it is important for the man to provide the frame and structure of a relationship when creating the kind of relationship that works for both parties involved. What can take away from the goal of forming a healthy relationship is unhealthy competition between spouses or partners. The goal in a relationship is to create and nurture connection and intimacy. Competition can act as either an interference or an obstacle. When fierce competition is present, it gets in the way and keeps one or both partners on the edge and defensive.*

Society has moved away from the traditional marriage roles upon which marriages in the past were created. Now new roles prevail, particularly when both spouses work. Men do better in relationships when their spouses help them organize their specific roles within the family. The man's role has become unclear as traditional roles have been lost within today's families. What is the direct result of these changes? Men are unable to pass strong examples of what it means to be the "man of the family" onto their sons, weakening even more with each generation.

When men are not sure of their own roles, they cannot pass on what seems unclear to them. A lack of clarity leads to a greater lack of clarity down the line.

As an example, imagine an assembly line comprised of many people, with each individual doing a different task, each working to achieve the same result – building a car that's meant to run. If just one person is out of sync on that assembly line and does not do the job that's expected, that car won't run efficiently. The same thing that can happen in an assembly line can happen in families when one or more in that family is out of sync with the others and does not do what others expect. The end product is not healthy. Expectations should be clear in order for members of the family to meet them.

DAY THREE: Missed steps... *ouch*!

TROY: "This morning, something wonderful and memorable happened for me during dance practice. It almost felt scary. When Jeni and I were dancing together, I was aware of a moment in which we really connected with each other. It was emotional for me, even a little electrifying, as we felt such intimacy. I looked into Jeni's eyes, searching for a cue to see if that feeling was there for her too. It was. It was at that moment that I knew we were in sync. We were in the groove. In that moment, I felt that everything was perfect...*that* is a moment I will never forget.

It was even more special to me because I shared it with Jeni. It made me feel "larger than life." I recalled how Jeni and I felt back in high school together, when we mutually revealed how much we cared for one another. That moment today was so special for me I thought, "I didn't know that I could feel that way again."

JENI: (morning) "We practiced a bit last night, starting and stopping and then restarting. Finally, we both felt as if we had hit a brick wall. If we continued to make the same mistakes, we would develop poor dance patterns that would continue into today's lesson. So, we decided it was best to stop and call it a night. We felt overwhelmed and were worried that when on our own, we seemed to forget everything we had learned on days one and two. While we felt so encouraged when we were dancing during class and felt we were taking command of our dancing ability, we now think, "not so much." Confidence is a fleeting thing...another lesson for the both of us. I wonder what today's lesson will hold for us?"

JENI: (evening) "Today in class, things felt good to me. I was excited when we found a song we both liked. The second part of that discovery happened when we moved around the dance floor together to this piece of music and we did it well. When we saw our reflections in the mirrors, we saw two happy people smiling back at us. It was just the two of us and we were even more motivated to be in the moment.

Troy told me he felt we "clicked." I was thrilled by how sweet he was when he shared that with me. I told him that I had felt the same way and agreed that it was a very special moment for me, too. It felt as if we were back on a date together. Then Troy choked up a little because this also represented a kind of breakthrough for him.

That moment of his revelation became even more exciting for me. I can't wait to see what tomorrow has in store for us – aside from the fact that I had already forgotten a step or two."

DAY FOUR: Breakfast before the last lesson

TROY: "This morning Jeni and I are sitting together on the last morning of our dance lessons. I'm being a little analytical, reviewing where we are in our learning curve. So far, we have had three lessons. This is the morning of our fourth and final lesson. I'm feeling anxious. Actually, if the truth were told, I'm freaking out a little. I'm concerned that I won't remember the dance steps. I'm sure I will feel embarrassed if I don't remember the steps. Then all this effort would have been wasted. There is that pride again.

I told Jeni that I am starting to see myself in a different way. I am shedding some of my old "emotional baggage" via the dance lessons. This has been an intense time for me – two hours daily – with each of us holding the other, touching each other and connecting with one another. This experience has been intense, soulful and deeply intimate.

I have been wondering how our lives may change from this point out. We'll be closer, I'm sure. I am looking forward to our days being filled with music and…I think there will be more touching, more passion for each other. I also expect that Jeni and I will enjoy the kind of connectedness that is emotional glue for a couple. I want more.

My feelings are now so intense that I hardly have words. Now we have the basic dance tools. We will have to commit to practice what we learned and remember what each of us needs from the other in order to make our dance together count.

For one fleeting moment, I thought about how easy it would be to quit but we both agreed to give it 100% of our effort. We had to go for it. I told myself to focus. I needed to achieve the end result of being able to dance."

JENI: "This morning, I am not sure I know how I feel. I hope I can remember what we were taught. But I'm also very excited about the steps we have taken both on and off the dance floor. We have learned a lot about each other and have created a nice foundation on which to build. I'm proud of Troy and I am impressed that he was willing to learn how to dance. From Troy's behavior and his words, I can see that he is anxious. I want and need to reassure him."

TROY: (evening) We just finished the last lesson. While I am relieved that the experience is behind us, I'm glad we did it. I can now put the tension behind me, too. It was a challenge for me to stay with it.

Our instructor, Darrel, told us that these lessons would be life changing. He was right. Before this trip when Jeni would ask me to dance with her, I would respond with, "Nah, I don't know how to dance." Now, it's different. Music makes us enjoy eye contact with one another. The difference is unbelievable.

There was an emotional moment when I broke down in tears. I am not sure what was going on but I had to stop dancing at one point. The feeling that surfaced was just too much. What I felt was an overpowering connection with Jeni.

JENI: (evening) "Darrel took a moment to remind us that we are dancing with a live human…our dance *partner*. We are not dancing with the mirrors or the floor. When I looked into Troy's eyes, I understood what the instructor was saying. It's about the connection with our partner that makes the dance go well or not. Troy and I have made real progress in this department. Now, not only do we "see" each other, but we also talk to one another as a new way of connecting. We were also reminded that our actions, gestures and movements all adjust according to the size of the person with whom we are dancing. Now, I am learning to feel comfortable and secure in Troy's arms.

Troy learned that he is the "frame." As the frame, his role is to fit to the size of his dancing partner, adjusting to her comfort. That would be me. He is supposed to feel that his arms fit his partner, something I find so appealing and is the reason I felt so supported by the "frame" he provided, once he got it right.

There was a very emotional moment when Troy broke into tears and we had to stop dancing. I felt it, too. It was an amazing sensation. It felt so good as we moved in time to the beat of the music. Everything seemed to come together for us. Then our eyes connected and at that personal moment, Troy was moved. Both of us were speechless.

I cried too. Here was our breakthrough. My husband had just come through a huge, twenty-some year battle over wanting to dance and not being able to, due to fears and inhibitions. When we were at that emotional moment, our instructor saw what happened and gave us a few moments knowing the significance of what just occurred. That is when Troy knew that the tools the instructor had given us would change our lives.

It was our "forever" moment and it was truly amazing. Troy told the instructor, "You did it. I get it now."

Troy and I now understand what this is all about. It is more far-reaching than just steps on a dance floor."

ERIK: *There is often a vast difference between what partners perceive as intimacy. One partner may grasp the feeling that emerges when they are dancing, describing this feeling as powerful, breathtaking and a consuming physical feeling when there is a real connection. Often, men don't get this. The stereotypical perspective is that most men equate intimacy with having sex and the physical expression of love. What a couple can discover together is that there are so many ways in which they can be intimate with one another...ways that do not include a sexual encounter. This kind of intimacy is deep. It feels very good. What we all long for is the intimacy we are talking about — vulnerability and closeness.* **That kind of intimacy has shelf life.**

A SUMMARY OF OUR DANCING EXPERIENCES

TROY: "Learning how to dance makes me want to continue dancing. Now, Jeni and I literally surround ourselves with music! It is a reminder that we need to keep dancing as a priority in our lives. When I hear music, I remember those wonderful feelings when Jeni and I were totally connected to one another. I want to relive that moment again and I want to feel that closeness again. Our love has deepened as the result of this experience. We promised each other to not let disagreements build up and not let small issues fester into larger ones. When disagreements escalate, we remind ourselves of "home base" so that those disagreements don't spill over into other parts of our lives."

JENI: "When we started this, we were not certain how the dancing lessons and the journal were all going to come together. Through our notes and the actual lessons, we have figured out that the man's role is very much the same in dancing as it is in real life. When dancing, it's the man's job to provide the structure, leadership and comfort. He provides the frame…supporting the woman's movements. I like Troy's taking that role in our relationship. When he leaves room for me to participate as a "partner" regarding major decisions and planning, I feel supported."

ERIK: *When the dance is in sync and when the relationship is healthy, a couple will move with each other, giving each other a frame of trust, support and connection. This is how to cultivate a healthy relationship with one another…on and off the dance floor.*

The analogy, "relationships are dances" is certainly powerful. The dance lessons were an effective tool for Troy and Jeni to understand more about their relationship and to discuss how they want their relationship to be. They were able to use dance as visualization.

To dance well, you must focus on your dance partner. You need to feel as if you are "one" with your dance partner. When you feel as "one," you both move with more fluidity and you are able to predict what your partner is going to do next. When you build relationships, you know it's working when you both gravitate together as a "we" and less of an "I." You then feel safe and vulnerable with your partner. When that relationship is healthy, you'll find that both you and your partner's needs are fulfilled. Like Troy and Jeni, you will experience a sense of closeness that you want and need.

If you are inspired to dance as the result of reading about Troy and Jeni's experience, then we encourage you to follow that inspiration. More importantly, we want you to be inspired by this analogy so that you use it to look at your own relationships and make the changes that can bring you happiness.

TAKE AWAY POINTS

- Be present in your interactions. To give vitality and meaning to the relationships in your life, you need to focus on the present.

- Remember that your relationships are dances. Each person in a relationship is equally responsible and accountable for the quality of that relationship. If it's not healthy, take the lead and change it.

- Discover your own "home base" and learn how and when to use it. Then, choose to use it.

- Don't stay stuck using the same dance steps. A shift in your focus and a fresh awareness will allow you to take the first step in choosing happiness.

- Don't waste your time or the time of others. Time is something you can't make up. Once the moments have ticked away, they are either used well or lost.

A WEDDING GIFT

When Troy and Jeni returned home from Las Vegas, they shared their story with Breezy, their daughter, and Drake, their future son-in-law. Breezy and Drake were excited to hear about their trip and the dance class. Jeni put on some classic rock music and both couples danced in the living room. Jeni watched Breezy's frustration grow as Breezy tried unsuccessfully to keep up with Drake.

Jeni and Troy, now armed with information, knew that this was not the way it should be. Troy waited for the dance to end and then explained to them the roles of the man and the woman in the dancing relationship. Troy told Drake, "Your role is to provide a solid frame for Breezy. You need to adjust your steps to accommodate her. Breezy cannot go as fast as you or take as many steps as you do and is not able to anticipate your moves, which makes her frustrated."

Breezy's frustration was because she could not keep up with Drake. She thought it was her fault and that she was a "poor dancer."

Drake took Troy's advice to heart and adjusted his dance to match her pace. Breezy began to feel more comfortable and supported in Drake's arms and felt happy to be an equal partner in the dance. Drake knew the dance moves and wanted to impress Breezy, but did not realize that he was supposed to be the framework and adjust to her. Breezy was unaware of her own role as well. The point of this story is that even though Breezy and Drake were dancing, the problem they were having was still a communication and connection issue. Drake thought his dance partner was there to keep up with him. Drake's take-a-way point from all this is the knowledge that they are a team.

Troy and Jeni gave their daughter and future son-in-law a valuable "pre-wedding" gift by sharing the lessons of their own dance experience. It was at Breezy and Drake's wedding that Troy raised a toast to them and said, "You are stronger together than you are as individuals. That is what you need to remember through your years of dancing together."

WHAT OBSTACLES STAND IN THE WAY OF YOUR HAPPINESS?

Imagine a brightly lit studio with a beautiful polished oak dance floor. We invite you and your partner to take a step onto that dance floor with us. We want you to feel the floor beneath your feet, listen for the beat of the music and be cognizant of the other dancers sharing the floor.

Now, imagine the other dancers as obstacles in your way forcing you to dance around them. They may brush up against you, get in your way or even collide with you. You have to take your attention away from your dance partner or you might misstep. This may cause your dance partner to misstep as well. Your attention and focus has now shifted from the dance you are doing with your partner. However, notice that these dancers/obstacles are not fixed and that you can navigate around them.

When you and your partner focus on each other and the dance, you are able to move around the floor with a common purpose. Just as you face obstacles on the dance floor, there are obstacles in your life. You can believe that those obstacles block your path or you can believe that they are simply something you can navigate around. Dances or relationships are improved when obstacles are not the focus.

OBSTACLE ONE
What's in it for me? How a "me first" philosophy could be the problem.

If it's "all about you" (as is often portrayed in the media and various forms of psychotherapy) and you agree with that philosophy, then why aren't you experiencing the high level of peace, contentment and satisfaction that you desire?

Here's why. It's time to dispel the myth that *"It's all about you."*

Would you be willing to consider that it's really about placing *your focus on others* rather than on yourself? Let's assume you believe in the "take care of myself-first" philosophy. We believe that this philosophy has evolved from the fear that if you don't put yourself first, no one else will.

Comfort can be found in the fact that you're not alone. In fact, you have a lot of company! From self-help materials that propagate "self-first," to politics and beyond, the media has done a thorough job of influencing the way society teaches us how to cultivate relationships.

The "me first" philosophy that "you need to make yourself happy before you can make anyone else happy" is severely flawed and irresponsible.

We believe that happiness is a by-product of lifting someone else up mentally, emotionally, physically and/or spiritually.

Lifting up someone else demands that you get outside of yourself. The best way to get outside of *you* is to be in the present and focus on something other than yourself! Be present to what is happening in someone else's world! It's time to start focusing on those around you.

We appreciate how hard it is to come home at the end of a busy, stressful day and have a genuine connection with spouses and children. Being present and emotionally available to those around us is hard, but not impossible. Being present means you are experiencing the moment rather than manipulating or controlling the mood and direction of that moment. Being present means you are choosing to focus on what is in front of your face.

Our emotional availability is the oxygen that feeds our relationships.

When you choose to not "get outside of yourself," you are operating from your emotions rather than from your intellect. When you are operating from your emotions, you are consumed with what you want and not with what is needed. These feelings are not about the other person or the situation. These feelings are about you. When you are consumed with your emotions, they are indeed that...*your* emotions. These emotions are not tagged to a situation or to other people. Instead, these emotions are all about you.

One therapeutic model explains this concept by using a line to illustrate the continuum between intellect and emotion. This continuum is used to show how each of us makes decisions based upon where our actions fall on that line. On average, most people will fall somewhere in the middle when they are feeling balanced.

Your thinking is likely to be healthier when you blend what you know to be right with an awareness of how you are feeling.

When we function primarily from our emotional perspective, we find crisis, chaos and drama as a natural part of our lives. Why? Emotions are inconsistent and unpredictable. The outcome of making our decisions based solely on our emotions is always crisis and chaos. When our actions are driven by emotion, we feel "this way" and "that way," and we are constantly being pulled in inconsistent directions. Inconsistency is a weak platform on which to build our lives. We are only as strong as what we stand on. The healthier we become, the more likely we will not base our decisions solely on our emotions.

On the other hand, when our actions are based entirely on intellect, we often lack intensity and passion. We don't love what we do, and typically, we do not *do* what we love.

The good news is that wherever you fall on the continuum whether it's the emotional side or the intellectual side, neither "landing" is permanent. Your life experiences and learning can alter where you are on this continuum and bring you closer to the middle and a more balanced life. In other words, your position on the continuum line is not permanent and can *always* be changed. Keep in mind that change can only happen with work, willingness and motivation.

Where are you are on the continuum? Draw a line and write the word "emotion" at one end and the word "intellect" at the other.

*Emotion*_____*Intellect*

Now, mark an "x" somewhere on the line showing where you are in your decision-making process. Do you find yourself leaning more toward the emotional side or the intellectual side?

Once you have an awareness of what drives your decision-making process, you will have a better understanding of where you want to be.

OBSTACLE TWO
Consumed with your past.

Learning to face forward is the first step in reaching your goal. Have you ever been successful at winning a race by running backwards? It's impossible!

Do you drive your car only focusing on the rear view mirror? You will definitely be able to focus on where you've been. However, it will be at the cost of you crashing in the present.

Are you constantly looking back, focusing on things that cannot be changed? By focusing on the past, you will continue to re-experience those same thoughts, emotions and fears as you relive those experiences that brought you pain and/or regret.

Learn how to face forward. It is imperative that you focus on *where you are going* rather than on where you have been.

> **ERIK:** *People consumed with their past are likely to be consumed with their pain and suffering. If it's true that our minds allow us to focus on only one state of mind at a time (past, present or future), why then would you choose to torture yourself by perpetuating your pain and suffering every day?*
>
> *Why focus on something that will never change? Instead, we can move through the pain when we choose to accept that the past will never change, no matter how long or how many times we look at it. Then, we can choose forgiveness and move on.*

OBSTACLE THREE
Body Armor – the invisible barrier

You can't see it and it's not like a piece of clothing.

Body armor is typically expressed in the form of anger. We choose to use it to avoid exposing our fears and/or hurts to other people. When we choose to not acknowledge and address our fears and/or hurts, we protect ourselves with anger.

While it may surprise you, initially, anger can have some positive qualities. When you feel angry, it comes from a place of choosing not to tolerate something. You are at the "end of your rope." For example, a mother living in an abusive situation might say, "I'm not going to let this happen to me anymore or to my child!" In this case, the anger is "self-preservation" anger. This kind of anger often fuels a person to create change.

When we use anger in an unhealthy manner, we are trying to deflect responsibility, look for blame and create hurt. This kind of anger keeps us fearful and separate from other people. It keeps us from resolving conflicts. Anger in this way becomes an invisible suit of armor. While "Body Armor" protects you, it may stop you from giving and receiving love. "Body Armor" keeps you from being genuine, authentic and vulnerable in your relationships. This obstacle will keep you from reaching the kind of joyful existence you desire.

If anger has been propelling your world, ask yourself if that anger is productive or if it is shielding you from being vulnerable and developing healthy relationships. If it is unhealthy anger, you might be missing opportunities that will bring you happiness and make your life healthier and more joyful.

REFLECT ON YOUR RELATIONSHIPS

The intensity of someone's anger is equal to the intensity of the fear and/or hurt that person is feeling. Our true colors are exposed when we are angry.

Anger is fear that is unaddressed or unacknowledged. It is like a heart attack.

When someone is having a heart attack, one of the first symptoms often signaling an attack is numbness in the left arm. The numbness will not go away until the heart attack is treated. The key is to focus on the problem rather than just treat the symptoms. In other words, the numb left arm represents *anger* and the heart attack represents the *hurt and/or fear*. Therefore, to cope with the anger, the hurt and fear must be acknowledged and addressed. If you don't address the numb left arm (anger), then the heart attack (fear and hurt) will consume you.

If you choose to continue to use Body Armor to protect yourself from feeling hurt again, you will be imprisoned by that hurt –perpetuating the exact emotion that you are trying to avoid. Your Body Armor will become the shield in which you house yourself and keep others at a distance.

Our Body Armor prevents us from being authentic, genuine and vulnerable in our relationships.

When you feel fearful or hurt, your perception is based upon an experience that you imagine will happen. Perhaps that feeling is based on something that has happened to you and that you believe has left you emotionally "scarred." You then become motivated by your experiences and your interpretation of those experiences.

Know that this is not who you are. Who you are is at that centered place that gives you a sense of balance. Who you are is at that place of love, compassion and wisdom within you. Who you are never changes but your interpretation of a situation *can* change.

ERIK: *Here's one such example. One day upon returning from school, my 8-year-old daughter, Olivia, said, "Today, my friend Ellie did not look at me all day and she would not play with me. I'm a bad friend. I'm not likeable."*

I responded by saying, "Liv, remember two nights ago when you were not very nice to Mom and me? Before you went to bed that night you said, "Oh guys, I'm sorry. It wasn't you. I was just feeling crummy about myself. I didn't mean to take it out on you guys. It really was me!"

So, let's follow that thought along. What if Ellie was having a bad day and she took it out on you like you did with your mom and me? What do you think?"

"Yeah, Dad, I never really looked at it that way. I understand now that it is not always about me and I don't always have to take it personally. Just because someone is angry with me doesn't always mean that I've done something wrong."

Liv got the lesson.

TROY: *While Erik and I are family, we are friends as well – friends who have always wanted to work together. What has always been powerful for me is that while we do not always agree with one another and do not always see things from the same perspective, we challenge and support each other. Our "dance" allows us to grow and become stronger as a result. What our relationship lacks is Body Armor, which is my point for sharing this story.*

OBSTACLE FOUR
When we hold negative beliefs about ourselves.

Sometimes we choose to believe positive things about ourselves because these positive thoughts make us feel good. Positive beliefs give us the self-confidence needed to be able to accomplish the things we want to do.

In contrast, there are the negative beliefs that destroy self-confidence, making us less likely to do the things we want to do or to meet the people we want to meet. Beliefs, both positive and negative, are difficult to change. If they've been around for a long time they become "habits". Unhealthy habits are hard to break. It's not impossible but to replace unhealthy habits with positive behavior does require work.

Here is another important rule. *We don't get what we want. We experience what we believe.* When our wants and our beliefs contradict each other, our beliefs will always trump our wants. Beliefs are so important that they are the foundation of what we create in our lives. If beliefs about ourselves are attached to negative past experiences and we don't move forward with new beliefs, we will end up editing our life story by putting a period where God intended to put a comma.

Here is a sampling of negative beliefs that hold us back from the life we want. Can you relate to any of the beliefs listed below?

> *"I'm not good enough."*
> *"I've done something wrong. I'm a bad person."*
> *"I don't deserve to be successful."*
> *"I should have done something else."*
> *"Men aren't successful at this...Women aren't good at doing that."*
> *"I don't deserve to be loved."*
> *"I'm not as good as..."*

If you choose to focus on and believe these negative thoughts, consider how every aspect of your life will be affected by this choice.

Beliefs drive actions – in either a healthy or an unhealthy way. Negative beliefs are an obstacle that prevent you from achieving the peace, contentment and satisfaction that you desire. Negative beliefs are limiting and self-sabotaging.

When you read Troy's story, you'll understand how the obstacle of negative beliefs impacted his life and may be affecting yours.

TROY'S WORRY STORY

Okay, so I was a worrier. Still am at times. I admit it. It all started when I was in college and I took a job selling health insurance to provide living expenses while I was in school. I lay awake every night worrying if I had left information off a health application, which would prevent the company from honoring a claim. I worried about making mistakes. I could not control the worry. Instead, it controlled my life. The worry was like a monster that threatened to come out of a closet. This "worry monster" ate up my sleep, night after night. I was a zombie.

For me, it was about the fear of making mistakes. I just worried about that possibility and what consequences would happen to clients as the result of my having "messed up." This problem became apparent when my employer started grooming me to be one of their sales leaders. Then, as quickly as they had their eye on me for leadership, the "other shoe fell" and I began to fall from grace. I was soon to be out of a job.

My regional Vice-President said, "Troy, I can't have you in this position. You worry too much and it shows. When you worry so much, your negative beliefs cut into your credibility. Because of your worry, you do not give the impression you have confidence and… frankly, it makes you appear weak. In fact, you look weak to me. And, if I can't count on you to be a strong individual, I can't have you in this job."

Oh, my gosh, I could not find words to respond. My confidence was shattered even more.

"Troy," he continued (as if I had not heard enough), "I am going to give you a piece of advice. Here is a study published in a self-help book. Basically, the study describes worry saying, 98% of the things we worry about never happen. 2% of the things that do happen are things you can handle."
He asked, "Troy, do you get up in the morning saying, 'Today is the day I will go to work to screw people?"

Sheepishly, I shook my head "no."

He continued, "Troy do you get up in the morning saying, 'Today I will take advantage of someone?'"

"No, that is not me," I answered. "I would never do that. I get up in the morning planning to do a good job. No one I know cares more than I do about doing a good job!"

"Well then, that's all that matters," he said. "You never try to take advantage of people. You try to do a good job and you focus on the people around you, more than on yourself. It's obvious to me that you care about the people whom you serve, and at the end of the day, you go to bed knowing you did the best job possible. Any worry past that, Troy, is a big waste of your time."

It was as if that Vice President just delivered the best sleeping potion. Right after that conversation, I started sleeping better. I knew I would not knowingly hurt anyone and I set my goals toward being in the present and producing good work.

ERIK: *When Troy chose to focus on the present, he essentially chose to not focus on and play out all the negative what-ifs – the 98%. The more Troy focused on the present, the more he believed in himself. It didn't take him long to realize that the more he believed in himself, the more everyone in his circle of influence was lifted up. Conversely, the more Troy's circle of influence was lifted up, the more it fed his belief in himself. This is the kind of experience that can be counted on to feed on itself.*

OBSTACLE FIVE
Financial and Economic Instability

It is an old truth: Money cannot guarantee happiness. But, having money can give a certain sense of freedom and choice.

In the 1990's people made money – lots of it, and very often spent far beyond their means. Many overextended themselves, abusing the concept of "credit." The public felt so confident about the flow of cash that they raised their "personal bar" even higher to compete with their neighbors. The same people who scrambled to buy a better car than the one their neighbors had, spent a large amount of time planning where to spend their cash and deciding what financial investments would have the largest return. Yet, the very thing that would provide the largest return – spending time with spouses and children – did not get the same emotional attention as their financial investments did.

Years later, the bottom fell out of the market and people found both themselves and the country deep in debt. The same people scrambling to keep up with others now found themselves struggling in a marketplace with fewer jobs. Not only were they out of work, they were also greatly in debt.

> **ERIK**: *Research tells us that the number one cause of divorce is financial problems. Financial issues are the leading cause of marital stress and conflict. "I can barely keep my head above water," is a phrase I hear almost daily. "I have to work more, have less free time, I'm making less money, I have less energy and I am scared," are more often stated phrases in therapy. Many are worried about having less time at home and fear the future. Isn't it odd that many of us are still spending our limited time worrying about financial stability instead of focusing on what will give us the greatest return and satisfaction... our families and our relationships?*

The question is, "What motivates you?" There will always be up and down cycles and changes in the economy. The key is to fasten your personal economic "seat belt" and change with the changes. Can you survive economic ups and downs? There will always be dynamic change but the ride will be less bumpy if you brace yourself with solid relationships.

An unpredictable economy is never a good thing and there are those who experience traumatic occurrences as a result. We are not, by any means, suggesting these difficult experiences won't happen. What we are saying is that the way you perceive the experiences will color what happens to you as a result of the negative experience. What we are also saying is that you should not motivate yourself based on your fear of what might happen. Instead, focus on the possibilities and on what you will learn.

> **ERIK**: *The only way a financial and economic barrier will remain a barrier to you is if you allow yourself to be motivated by it. It will still exist. However, it is how you respond to it that will drive what happens to you.*

> **TROY**: *Here is another reason to see economic instability as an obstacle that can be navigated around versus an impenetrable wall. For example, your boss might be looking for someone who can see above the situation, maintain a good attitude and be an example for others to follow. The situation may prove to be an opportunity to promote yourself by shining in spite of adversity and by being a positive example for others. This is called leadership.*

Other people cannot see inside you. They only see what you show them. It is attitude that wins each time. Who knows what the future has in store? Each time you demonstrate attitude and behavior, you are seeding the garden for your future. Do you want your garden to come up with wild weeds or healthy, strong and resilient plants?

OBSTACLE SIX
Revenge and Injustice.

Revenge and injustice are the two main obstacles that stop us from forgiving someone. Forgiveness allows us to "move on" from a bad experience. Choosing not to forgive keeps us focused on the past.

Revenge, (*I want you to feel and know how much pain you have caused me and how much you have affected my life*), is a huge obstacle to navigate around. Injustice, (*I don't think this is fair*), is another mountain to climb on the way to forgiveness.

When you feel so angry that you cannot forgive, you want revenge. You are motivated, actually driven, by injustice. When your thoughts about revenge overwhelm you with thoughts of, "It just isn't fair," it is the injustice that traps you. The reason? You are focusing on the past and not on the present, where you can find balance and peace.

Why should you forgive…and how?

People have a very difficult time with forgiveness, often mistaking it for permissiveness, even weakness. This type of forgiveness does not have to be verbalized to the other person. Often this type of forgiveness can be better understood when thinking of it "as acceptance."

"I forgive you because I choose to not carry this burden around anymore. The energy it takes from me to focus on the situation is at the cost of me being in the present. Since I cannot be in the past and the present at the same time… I choose the present."

What's getting in the way of your forgiveness? *Perhaps it is the direction of your feet.* Turn around, stop focusing on the past and face forward.

Choosing not to forgive keeps you tethered to your past. Focus on the present instead. It is important that you are genuine and put your energy toward the present, making that your motivation.

Do not turn back and focus on the object of your anger, the things that person did and how it made you feel. If you do focus on how powerless, how victimized, how helpless, how hurt you felt, how do you think those thoughts will motivate you? What is the "you" that you will be projecting to others?

What you focus on will motivate you. And, what motivates you is what you focus on.

Being unable to forgive is a barrier as it keeps you stuck in the past. You won't be able to move forward. You can't move on with your life. It stops you from grieving the losses. As long as you focus on the feeling of injustice or revenge, you will not be able to grieve in a healthy or timely manner. You will remain stuck.

How big is this issue of concentrating on where you want to place your focus? It is monumental.

It is your decision. You can close this chapter with the feeling that your anger is too great and is worth the energy you are putting towards it.

On the other hand, you can accept what has happened to you as unchangeable and is no longer worth focusing on at the cost of your peace, contentment and satisfaction.

What will you choose?

Our profound message to you...

You can choose to believe that you do have the ability to navigate around all your obstacles.

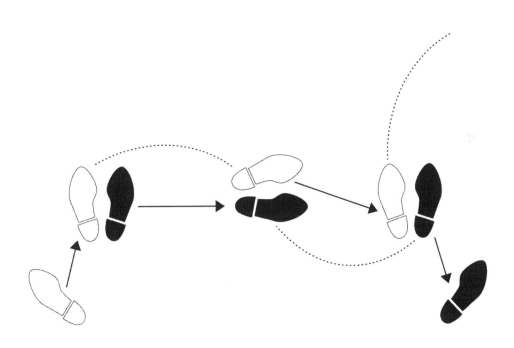

ERIK'S CABIN STORY

This is a story about my friend, Gray…a risk taker who taught me a life-changing lesson. Gray is a therapist like me. He participates in bike races down steep mountain slopes, such as Breckenridge and Telluride. In the spring and summer, Gray bikes these slopes regularly, citing the thrill of "flying down the mountains."

There came a time when I told Gray, "You know, I want to do this, too." Gray's first reaction was to chuckle. Then, seeing how serious I was, he offered to take me with him.

We arrived at our perfect place. As we stood at the top of the mountain, I screamed, "Holy Cow! It's steep!! I can't believe you guys fly down this racing each other to the bottom." I saw the huge boulders, trees and jagged tree stumps that Gray had warned me about on our drive up the mountain. I didn't know how I was going to navigate around all those obstacles.

Gray told me to get on my bike and buckle up. He told me that I could not use my brake, because if I did, I would fishtail and lose control. "You just have to go for it. Okay, go ahead!"

There I was, the first time going downhill. I noticed an eighteen-inch gap between some boulders and tree stumps that Gray pointed out. I felt like I was flying. I saw one boulder, then another, and another and then…bam, I hit a boulder! I flew off my bike and landed on the ground. I knew I had to get back on. Gray, smiled and chuckled, and then he began laughing... loudly...and I was getting angry. "Okay," I told him, "I am not going to focus on the boulder." I pointed to the tree stump. "I need to make it right between the tree stump and the boulder."

Once again, Gray yelled out, "Go for it." I started downhill focused and determined on not hitting the tree stump. Bam...I hit the tree stump. And once more, I flew off my bike. This time, my nose was bleeding. Gray was laughing so hard he had trouble catching his breath. By this time, I was developing a lot of humility along with the frustration that accompanies failure.

"Have you had enough?" asked Gray. And I said, "Okay, yeah!"

Then Gray said, "See the cabin at the bottom of the hill?" Yeah...I saw it. It was the size of a dime from where we were standing.

Gray became serious. "That needs to be where your focus is. That is exactly what you should focus on as you are flying down the mountain, Erik, because I assure you that you will hit whatever you focus on. Your brain processes faster than you think it does."

I found what he said hard to believe. I wondered how a person could make it through the gaps by not focusing on them. I felt humble and a little beat up, but thought I would try it his way.

I focused on the cabin as Gray said and I felt like a "rock star" swishing through those little gaps. I was amazed! I told Gray that I wished a few more of my friends could have seen me. "This is incredible," I told him. "I was totally in the zone on the way down." I paused, "There was this perfect moment when I knew I was on the right path and that felt so good."

That night when we were at the campsite, sitting by the fire, we once again became two therapists talking. You can imagine that with two therapists the conversation was getting very deep. We both were thinking that this whole experience is such a great metaphor for living life.

I opened up, talking about myself and how often I wake up thinking about all the possible obstacles that present themselves in my daily life. *I have this client to keep safe...I have these financial demands to meet...Can I find enough time to call my colleagues back*, etc. I also focus on all the various things that could potentially derail me from parenting my teenage daughters in a safe and healthy manner. Then, it hit me. The same process that I applied on the bike trail to reach the cabin can be applied to my life as well.

I wondered, what is my personal cabin? What do I need to focus on in my daily life that will allow me to navigate around the obstacles I am facing? That was a pivotal moment for me. *Where am I heading?*

Our ultimate cabin is happiness. Not just the kind of happiness that puts a smile on your face but the type of happiness you experience from successfully navigating through the obstacles in your day. This allows you to lay your head down on your pillow that night feeling peace, contentment and satisfaction with your choices.

CABINS can represent:

- **Choosing courage over fear.**
- **Choosing to focus on forgiveness versus injustice and revenge.**
- **Choosing to love people in your life and allowing them to love you.**
- **Choosing to notice what you *do* have versus what do not have.**
- **Choosing to face forward and not focus on the past.**

When we focus on the cabin, the obstacles will not go anywhere. They will still be there, like the tree stumps. I am not telling you that by thinking wonderful things your obstacles will magically disappear. They won't. What I am saying is the same thing I learned. Your brain effortlessly navigates you around your obstacles when you focus on your target...your cabin.

We want to help you see and understand what may be acting as a barrier/obstacle in your life. When you face an obstacle that looms large, it can force you to accept certain behaviors as "it's just the way I am." Thus, obstacles serve as an excuse for staying stagnant and not making changes. We want you to see obstacles as something you can navigate your way around...versus merely accepting them as a part of who you are.

We are walking the same walk with you. We face the same obstacles. It's not like our lives are any easier to get through. It's just that we have learned not to put a lot of emphasis on the obstacles.

That is our message to you. Shift your emphasis off the obstacles and place your focus on the tools that we are going to share with you in the upcoming chapters. These tools will help you find the peace, contentment, and satisfaction you desire.

You have the power to choose which thoughts you want to focus on and feed. That is your power. One of life's greatest secrets is to see obstacles as something you can navigate your way around rather than as fixed barriers blocking your happiness.

SITTING IN ON A THERAPY SESSION
WITH ERIK

I start my therapy sessions by asking, "What would need to happen so that at the end of our therapeutic relationship, you would be able to say, 'This was awesome'.

I want this to be worth your time, your money and your energy. I want you to feel comfortable referring me to the people that you care about. I want this process to genuinely impact your lives. And, I want to do this in a very authentic way.

I want to be able to run into you five years from now and know that the experience was genuine and solid and that you are still using the tools you learned. That becomes my cabin.

Let's go back to where we began in our session and talk about your cabin in therapy. What would need to happen for you to walk away from this therapeutic relationship believing the experience was worth your time, your money and your energy? Essentially, that becomes your cabin in therapy."

In closing, I say, "You all have done a great job telling me about what brought you here...describing what's frustrating you. I'm impressed with your ability to clearly talk about your frustrations. Not only have you come into therapy – a big move – but you also have clearly taken the initiative to create change.

Part of my job is to get you to do things that you normally would not do, right? What I want to do is to 'turn you around' so that each of you stops focusing on all the things you have just listed for me. By 'turning you around,' you will be facing forward, not backward. You are more loving, you are smarter, you are a better problem-solver, and you are stronger when you are facing forward.

Let me tell you that it's much easier, when running a race, to do it facing forward! I want you to run this race...this process of therapy...facing forward. Part of the exercise and reason for facing forward is that we need to have a direction. We need a target/finish line. We need to have a thing that we are heading toward. And just like the cabin in my cabin story, this will be one of your cabins."

WHAT ARE YOUR PERSONAL CABINS?

You've learned that it's all about aim and focus. It's all coming together, right here. We will teach you how to choose healthy cabins. We'll give you a special "lens" to improve your clarity. Our goal is to lead you on a healthy and successful journey that will help satisfy your hunger for happiness.

It is important that your cabins be healthy from all four perspectives – mental, physical, emotional and spiritual. Make sure that what you have declared as your cabin is not at the expense of someone else's mental, emotional, physical or spiritual wellbeing.

When you focus on your cabins, and those cabins are healthy on all levels, you will be energized! You will experience a sense of peace, contentment, and satisfaction.

Let's imagine for a moment that while you are sleeping all the barriers that stop your relationships from reaching a place of peace, contentment and satisfaction are suddenly gone. You wake up and realize that during the night all of your barriers have vanished.

How would this experience influence your thoughts, emotions and perceptions for the coming day?

- Would your relationship with your significant other be an equal partnership?
- Would your significant other feel loved and supported by you?
- Would your significant other say that you are stronger together than when you are apart?
- Would your children see you as a consistent, loving and predictable parent?
- Would your children describe you as being emotionally available and safe to be around?
- Would your coworkers say that you contribute more than you take?
- Would your coworkers see you as a team player?
- Would your friends see you as someone who undoubtedly has their back?

ERIK: *It has been my experience over the years and in many counseling settings that people have trouble verbalizing what it is that they do want. It's also evident that many people have difficulty describing where they are going or knowing when they get there. Typically, people don't recognize their own markers for achievement. It's hard to work toward a goal if you don't know or can't describe how it would feel when you reach that goal. Finding these answers requires you to focus on where you want to go versus focusing on where you don't want to go. Our visualization question is a great approach to helping people define their cabins.*

TROY: *I've attended many sales/self-help seminars and listened to presenters talk about how to define goals and objectives for a successful and fulfilling life. Their strategies were so vague that I could never quite grasp, nor could I apply, the principals that they were trying to teach. I could never define and hang onto the desired goals and objectives I wanted to accomplish with their techniques.*

Erik's Cabin Story allows me to focus on those relationships that are crucial to my success and happiness. I am able to visualize just how I want each relationship to look. I am able to focus on what I need to do to create that healthy cabin with each person. By focusing on that healthy cabin/relationship with each person, I can navigate around whatever obstacles I might encounter.

WHAT DO YOU WANT TO SEE INSIDE
EACH OF YOUR CABINS?

With each of the cabins you choose, it is important that your intentions and thoughts are positive, loving, nurturing and uplifting. You will find that bad/negative or sabotaging thoughts will weaken and destroy your cabins. The following story illustrates that you do have a choice about what you choose to focus on.

ERIK : *Defining your cabin involves more than visualizing what you want each relationship in your life to look like. This is when your imagination and your intentions overlap. Be clear with your intention and then imagine applying that intention to the relationship. What are your intentions for each relationship? How would that look and how would people be affected?*

Cabins can be "short term" cabins, "long term" cabins or even a cabin big enough to hold other cabins.
- ✓ *My "marriage" cabin would encompass my "children" cabin as well as my "family" cabin.*
- ✓ *It also encompasses my cabin that represents my relationship with God, which in turn, encompasses all my other relationships.*

TROY: First, I don't strive for just ONE cabin. My life is filled with "individual" cabins that are tied to each relationship within my life. Some are "short term" cabins while others are "long term" cabins.

I start by defining the most important cabins –the ones with my family. I make sure that each cabin is built on a healthy supportive relationship. I see myself looking in that cabin window visualizing how I want each relationship to look. I know it has to be healthy on all levels. This is where I want to be...mentally, spiritually, physically and emotionally.

At the end of each day, if I have not created a healthy cabin for each person, then I change it. I monitor my "individual" cabins each day so I can get back on track if I'm unhappy with where I am with each one. Then tomorrow, my focus will be on rebuilding that cabin so it is healthy.

In all of these areas, each day is made up of my actions that will either make for a healthy cabin or an unhealthy cabin. It is my choice. Here are some of my cabins that I focus on:

- ✓ My wife, Jeni: that she feels supported and lifted up by me; and that she is an equal partner in our marriage.

- ✓ My son, Bryce, and his wife, Renee: that they feel supported and lifted up by me; and that they will use me as a foundation to establish their new life together.

- ✓ My daughter, Breezy, and her husband, Drake: that they feel supported and lifted up by me; and that they can count on my support and love as they build their life and careers.

- ✓ My customers: that I strive to give each customer individualized service so that I can meet their varied needs; and that I am an asset to them in performing their business activities.

- ✓ Bear Graphics, my business: that my overall success in business is based on utilizing all the tools at my disposal to maintain healthy cabins with each of my customers.

THE STORY OF TWO WOLVES
A Cherokee Proverb

One evening an old Cherokee told his grandson a story about a battle that goes on inside all people. He said, "My son, the battle is between two 'wolves' inside us all."

"One wolf is evil. It is anger, envy, jealousy, sorrow, regret, greed, arrogance, self-pity, guilt, resentment, inferiority, lies, false pride, superiority, and ego."

"The other wolf is good. It is joy, peace, love, hope, serenity, humility, kindness, benevolence, empathy, generosity, truth, compassion and faith."

The grandson thought about it for a minute and then asked his grandfather: "Which wolf survives?"

The old Cherokee simply replied, "The one you feed."

This story is a personal favorite of Erik's. He tells clients that whatever thoughts they feed are the ones that survive. It's all part of an overall process. It's up to each one of us to decide which thoughts we want to focus on. Why would we want to feed and focus on fearful and unhealthy thoughts?

Which thoughts do you want to see survive and become an integral part of the path to your cabin? It's your responsibility to feed those healthy thoughts.

Be mindful and thoughtful about where you choose to place your focus, and know that whatever you focus on will be what you feed.

BUILDING YOUR CABIN'S
FOUNDATION WITH CHARACTER

The longevity of each cabin is contingent on the strength of your cabin's foundation. A foundation is important in building a cabin designed to last. Likewise, a foundation is important in building a life that has meaning. Building the foundation of a house begins with laying rebar – connecting metal rods in a checkerboard fashion to support the concrete when it hardens. The rebar is what gives the concrete foundation strength and form. Figuratively speaking, character is the rebar that gives a person a strong foundation in building a meaningful life.

It is not always obvious by looking at the outside of a foundation whether or not it contains rebar. However, when a poorly built foundation experiences an inevitable, unexpected shift, the house built on it weakens creating severe structural damage.

When a family's foundation is weak, it usually lacks the "rebar" or the "character strengths" to weather life's storms. The old adage, "Murphy's Law", says "anything that can go wrong will go wrong". Life challenges come in clusters. Life tends to toss new challenges at us before we have managed to resolve the present one. Some events are so difficult we feel as if we cannot handle one more crisis! Then, something else happens to further disrupt things, adding more pressure and stress.

When this happens, the "foundation" of the family is either strong enough to withstand crisis or it becomes severely weakened, causing the family structure to crumble. The condition of the foundation is a primary factor.

Character strengths and virtues are interchangeable. Aristotle's description of virtue is, "a balanced point between a deficiency and an excess of a trait. The point of the greatest virtue lies not in the exact middle but at a golden mean, sometimes closer to one extreme than the other."

For example:

COURAGE
is the mean (average) between cowardice and fool heartedness.

CONFIDENCE
is the mean (average) between self-depreciation and vanity.

GENEROSITY
is the mean (average) between sharing and giving, and selfishness.

Further, Aristotle says, "*It is excellence at being human – (virtue is) a skill which helps a person survive (trials), for meaningful relationships and finding happiness. Learning (virtues) is usually difficult at first, but it becomes easier when practiced over time until it becomes a habit.*"

You get the idea. It's about balance and common sense!

VIRTUE AND CHARACTER

Erik has a diverse practice. One large segment of his practice involves families. One of the other practice segments involves the counseling of high-risk adolescent boys. Typically, these boys are placed in a special residential facility by the court, which for some may be the last stop before incarceration. The residential facility is small and has a team of specialized professionals. The residents and their families learn to develop new pathways of thinking, behaving and perceiving.

> **ERIK:** *One of the techniques I teach in this type of situation is how to make healthy choices, which I believe is a learned skill. It is often the boys' lack of ability in this department that got them to this point in the first place. We talk about making decisions from a more "centered" place in their thinking. It is in that "centered place" where love, compassion and wisdom can be found. Then, intellect can be balanced with emotions. In addition, and equally as important, is the fact that in the center of it all is what we call "character."*
>
> *What most people lack, and especially these young men, is balance and character. When I'm working in a group setting, I often present this concept. I tell the boys that there are times in life when things seem to be going well. From an outside perspective, it may even seem we are just cruising through life. Things look easy. Then I explain that we get to see what we are really made of when we hit speed bumps or potholes along the way.*
>
> *I add that this is actually an exciting opportunity! Will they choose resiliency? Will they choose courage? The boy's spirits are renewed with hope when I remind them they now have an opportunity to choose courage and raise themselves up!*
>
> *I tell them, "Some of you will choose courage and some of you are not willing to choose courage right now. However, each of you can choose courage at <u>any time</u> during this experience. This is an opportunity for you to strengthen your personal foundation with character."*

THE DIFFERENCE BETWEEN
MEN AND BOYS

Becoming a man does not coincide with reaching a certain age. Being a man for these adolescents means that when they hit speed bumps, they get to decide how they want to deal with them – with or without character. Being a man is the crossover bridge to thinking and acting with character.

Erik enjoys using metaphors in his counseling groups to illustrate his teaching points. He calls this one *"Getting Hit by the Pitch."*

A guy goes up to bat and gets hit by a pitch. He drops down, stays down and takes himself out of the game. He lets everybody know that he was the guy who got hit with the pitch and had to leave the game.

Or...consider the guy who gets hit by the pitch. He's hurt. Instead of taking himself out of the game, he brushes himself off and takes his base. This *guy is operating from character/courage. If he functions only from emotion, he will function out of fear. So, why would a guy stay in the game after he just got hit with a ninety mile per hour fast ball? He would stay in the game...but only if he chooses character/courage which allows him to move forward from that experience.*

When someone steps back up to the plate after being hurt, that person is functioning from character and courage. You can choose to get up. You can start again. You can step back into life! *You can be resilient*!

WHAT'S AHEAD?

We have developed a toolbox that we call **The Timeless Twenty Toolkit**©. We've filled it with "character tools" that will help you strengthen your cabin's foundation. These tools will also help guide you toward your cabin and steer you toward healthier relationships and a fulfilling and happy life.

Part II

THE TIMELESS TWENTY TOOLKIT ©

Do you crave more peace, contentment and satisfaction in your life? Are you ready to learn how to navigate around life's obstacles?

The **Timeless Twenty Toolkit**© is a set of "character" tools that will help guide you toward your cabin and steer you toward healthier relationships and a fulfilling and peaceful life. In this section, we introduce you to 20 *time-tested* tools that we guarantee will change your perceptions and your life – *if you choose to use them consistently.*

We invite you to pick up your toolkit and fill it with the most valuable and priceless tools you will ever use to build the life you've always wanted!

When I grew up in Chicago in the 80's, we didn't have a Home Depot. Now, I live in a small town in western Colorado and it excites me to no end that we have a Home Depot! I love walking down aisles looking at the hundreds of tools that are available. I often catch myself saying, "I didn't know they made a tool for that!" or "I think I can build that!" More often than not, I leave the store with a new project in mind and a tool or two in my bag.

I believe that counseling should be like an emotional "Home Depot." My intention is for people to leave our sessions saying, "I didn't know there was a tool for that." and "I think I can do that!" I want my clients to leave the session feeling inspired, excited, motivated and capable to achieve the change they desire.

I explain that my job as a therapist is to introduce the client to new tools, teach them how to use those tools, and help them to become skilled at using them. Their job is to use the tools in between our sessions, come back, and tell me which tools are a good fit for them and their family and which ones are not. Then, we can swap out tools, "two- for-one," until we find the right tools that are tailored specifically for them.

The intention of this book is to show you the top twenty tools that I have seen individuals, couples and families benefit from the most. These twenty tools have a 100% guarantee. The Timeless Twenty Toolkit© will work every time you use it because it is consistent and predictable. The Timeless Twenty Toolkit© creates peace, contentment and satisfaction in all of your relationships, and ultimately, in you.

These character tools absolutely do have a 100% guarantee. They will work every time you use them. The only reason they will not work is if you let the little sabotaging voices in your head convince you they won't. It is important for you to know that we all have these same little voices trying to sabotage us. They say things like "This won't work." "You can't do that!" "How will people respond to that?" "You're a fake and everyone is going to find out!"

These are false statements. They are not real. This is where your mind goes if you are not focusing on the present. I believe you do have the ability to focus on positive and productive thoughts rather than the dark destructive thoughts that we all have.

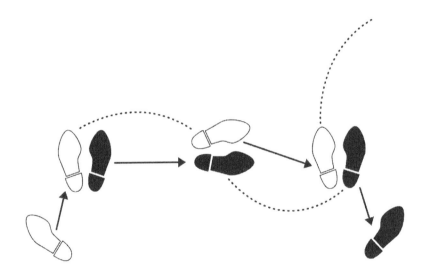

GRATITUDE

Gratitude is synonymous with thankfulness and appreciation. It is an attitude and acknowledgment of a benefit that one has received or will receive. Gratitude is not merely feeling grateful, but it is a choice to be motivated by that gratitude to do something outside of yourself.

We believe that feeling and showing gratitude is critically linked to our mental health. Studies show that when we express gratitude, our overall quality of life and well-being benefit significantly. We have found that the best way to begin to acknowledge and show gratitude is by keeping a daily journal listing the things for which we are grateful. A simple way to begin using this tool is to list three things daily that you choose to be grateful for. We are confident that once you start this process, you will notice a positive impact on your attitude, relationships and daily life.

WHY PRACTICE GRATITUDE?

Over the past decade, hundreds of studies have documented the social, physical, and psychological benefits of gratitude. The research suggests these benefits are available to most anyone who practices gratitude, even in the midst of adversity. Here are some of the top research-based reasons for practicing gratitude.

- Gratitude brings us happiness: In research by Robert Emmons, happiness expert, Sonja Lyubomirsky[3], and many other scientists, practicing gratitude has proven to be one of the most reliable methods for increasing happiness and life satisfaction; it also boosts feelings of optimism, joy, pleasure, enthusiasm, and other positive emotions.
- Gratitude reduces anxiety and depression.
- Gratitude is good for our bodies: Studies by Emmons and his colleague Michael McCullough suggest gratitude strengthens the immune system, lowers blood pressure, reduces symptoms of illness,

---

[3]http://greatergood.berkeley.edu/topic/gratitude/definition-46k-Robert Emmons: Benefits of Gratitude. The Greater Good Science Center/University of California/Berkeley

and makes us less bothered by aches and pains. It also encourages us to exercise more and take better care of our health.

- Grateful people sleep better: They get more hours of sleep each night, spend less time awake before falling asleep, and feel more refreshed upon awakening. If you want to sleep more soundly, count blessings, not sheep.
- Gratitude makes us more resilient: It has been found to help people recover from traumatic events, including Vietnam War veterans with PTSD.
- Gratitude strengthens relationships: It makes us feel closer and more committed to friends and romantic partners. When partners feel and express gratitude for each other, they each become more satisfied with their relationship. Gratitude may also encourage a more equitable division of labor between partners.
- Gratitude promotes forgiveness.
- Gratitude makes us "pay it forward": Grateful people are more helpful, altruistic, and compassionate.
- Gratitude is good for kids: When 10-19 year olds practice gratitude, they report greater life satisfaction and more positive emotions, and they feel more connected to their community.
- Gratitude is good for schools: Studies suggest it makes students feel better about their school; it also makes teachers feel more satisfied and accomplished, and less emotionally exhausted, possibly reducing teacher burnout.

I believe gratitude is looking at my life and knowing that I have enough. Choosing gratitude demands that I am in the moment. Being grateful is my opportunity to get connected with God. I believe our deepest sense of gratitude comes through grace. It is an awareness that we have not earned, nor do we deserve, what we have been given. When people desire a connection with God and those around them, gratitude is the vehicle. When I am grateful, I know I have had nothing to do with the reason for my gratitude. I am grateful I have what I have. Gratitude is a whole paradigm shift. It's the ability to see what I have and to not focus on that which I do not have.

Choosing gratitude is all-important. I think all of us should begin and end each day with gratitude. This is something I have tried to instill in my children.

GAUGING YOUR GRATITUDE
Where do you measure up?

> **FAR LEFT (RED ZONE): YOU ARE NOT GRATEFUL.**

- You are unappreciative.
- You are insatiable, unable to be satisfied.

> **THE MIDDLE (GREEN ZONE): YOU FOCUS ON HAVING GRATITUDE.**

- The healthy balance of feeling appreciation and being able to express that appreciation in a genuine way.

> **FAR RIGHT (RED ZONE): YOU USE GRATITUDE IN AN UNHEALTHY WAY.**

- You use gratitude as a means of seeking attention.
- You fake being grateful to gain other people's approval.

CONSIDER THIS!

 You can make personal changes in two ways. You can either let your head lead and your heart will follow or you can let your heart lead and your head will follow. Here is an idea to consider. Let's say you are not genuinely choosing gratitude but act grateful anyway. Would you begin to eventually experience genuine gratitude? Absolutely. Sometimes a little "acting" is in order and we need to "fake it 'til we make it".

It is evidenced-based that simply focusing on gratitude will lower your blood pressure as well as your heart rate. Research also shows choosing to use gratitude strengthens your immune system. Gratitude has the power to heal, energize and change lives. Knowing this information, why would anyone choose not to use this tool?

What works for me and has turned into a "must-use" tool in my everyday toolbox is this: by encouraging yourself to reach out to others to show gratitude, you will create an immediate response of kindness back to you. It becomes a circle of love that always begins with you showing gratitude to someone else first.

IF I WERE GRATEFUL RIGHT NOW (If I was able to notice what I *do* have in my life versus what I *don't* have in my life) I WOULD BE GRATEFUL FOR.....

② SOCIAL AWARENESS

Having a healthy amount of social awareness is necessary both on a personal and professional level. The competencies associated with being socially aware are:

- **EMPATHY**: understanding the other person's emotions, needs and concerns.
- **SERVICE**: the ability to understand and meet the needs of others.
- **ORGANIZATIONAL AWARENESS**: the ability to understand the politics of working within organizations.

Essentially, awareness of social situations is about carefully considering what people want and planning to communicate with them in a way that is intended to meet that need. Great leaders and public speakers are skilled in this ability and it helps them build support. At its worst, social awareness can be calculating and manipulative. At best, being socially aware is a natural response to people, taking their situation and needs into account as much as possible.

Dr. Alan Zimmerman[4] writes: One young man had to learn that the hard way, as my friend Palani at PAL Vision Associates told me. He told me about a young man who went to apply for a managerial position in a big company. He passed the initial interview, and now he was about to meet the director for his final interview. The director discovered from his resume that the youth's academic achievements were excellent. He asked, "Did you obtain any scholarships in school?" The young man answered "no".

"Was it your father who paid for your school fees?"

"My father passed away when I was one year old. It was my mother who paid for my school fees." he replied.

"Where did your mother work?" The young man said, "My mother worked as a clothes cleaner."

---

[4] Dr. Alan Zimmermans's Tuesday Tip #675, May 20, 2013 www.drzimmerman.com

The director asked the job applicant to show him his hands. The applicant showed his that were smooth and perfect. So, the director asked, "Have you ever helped your mother wash the clothes?"

"Never, my mother always wanted me to study and read more books. Besides, my mother can wash clothes faster than me." said the young man.

The director said, "I have a request. When you go home today, go and clean your mother's hands, and then see me tomorrow morning." The young man felt that his chance of landing the job was high. When he went back home, he asked his mother to let him clean her hands. His mother felt strange, but with mixed feelings, she showed her hands to her son.

The young man cleaned his mother's hands slowly, with tears dripping down his face. It was the first time he noticed that his mother's hands were so wrinkled and so covered in bruises. Some bruises were so painful that his mother winced when he touched them.

This was the first time the young man realized that it was this pair of hands that washed clothes every day to pay for his education. After cleaning his mother's hands, the young man quietly washed all the remaining clothes for his mother. That night, the mother and son talked for a very long time.

The next morning, the young and eager job applicant went to the director's office. The director noticed the tears in the applicant's eyes when he asked, "Can you tell me what you learned at your house yesterday?"

The young man answered, "I cleaned my mother's hands, and I finished cleaning all the remaining clothes. I know now what appreciation is. Without my mother, I would not be who I am today. By helping my mother, I not only realized how difficult it is to get something done on your own, but I also have come to appreciate the importance and value of helping other people."

The director said, "This is what I am looking for in a manager. I want to recruit a person who can appreciate the help of others, a person who knows the sufferings of others to get things done, and a person who would not put money as his only goal in life. You are hired!"

The new manager worked very hard and received the respect of his subordinates. Every employee worked diligently and worked as a team. The company's performance improved tremendously. All because this new manager had gained a significant portion of Social Awareness.

As a footnote, let me tell you that a child who is protected and habitually given whatever he wants, develops an "entitlement mentality" and will always put himself first. He would be ignorant of his parent's efforts. When he starts work, he would assume that every person must listen to him, and when he becomes a manager, he would never know the sufferings of his employees and would always blame others when things don't go his way.

A child raised this way may be good academically, and successful for a while, but eventually he would not feel a sense of achievement. He will grumble, be full of hatred, and fight for me-me-me.

You can let your child live in a big house, eat a good meal, learn piano, and watch TV on a big screen. But if you want to raise social awareness in your kids, when you are cutting grass, let them experience it as well. After a meal, let your children wash their plates and bowls together with their brothers and sisters. Let your kids know that even though you could afford a maid, you may not have one…because you want your children to experience the difficulty of learning how to work with others to get things done.

 I believe social awareness is the character tool that bridges my mental intellect to my everyday life, and most importantly into my relationships. It allows me to do something with what I know.

 I believe the social awareness tool can only be used when you connect with people. The best way to begin connecting with people is to start asking questions about things they care about such as their children, their family, and their work. Social awareness begins with genuinely listening and responding to what they say.

GAUGING YOUR SOCIAL AWARENESS
Where do you measure up?

FAR LEFT (RED ZONE): YOU ARE NOT SOCIALLY AWARE.

- You are self-centered.
- You do not have the ability to "read" others. You lack the ability to understand and interpret what's going on around you.
- You do not step outside of yourself to understand what motivates and drives others.

THE MIDDLE (GREEN ZONE): YOU UNDERSTAND THE EMOTIONS, NEEDS AND CONCERNS OF OTHERS.

- You are aware of the motives and feelings of other people.
- You do what is right in order to fit into different situations and with different people.
- You have the ability to put people at ease.
- You have the ability to "read" social cues and to use this information to guide what you do and say.
- You know your limits with different people and show respect for those who hold beliefs that differ from yours.
- You are not contentious, nor do you seek ways to irritate people or see how far you can push others.

FAR RIGHT (RED ZONE): YOU USE SOCIAL AWARENESS AS A MEANS TO MANIPULATE.

- Your social awareness is motivated by self-centered purposes.
- You are able to "read" people but are too much of a "people pleaser."

- You try to please and agree with everyone at the cost of losing your own thoughts, emotions and perceptions.

CONSIDER THIS!

 When you choose social awareness, you know what to do and say in different situations and you do it well. With this tool, you know how to align your actions to meet each social situation so that you are appropriate.

 I like the adage "You have two ears and one mouth, which means you should listen twice as much as you speak." Social awareness begins with listening to those around you and then responding to their needs.

 I AM SOCIALLY AWARE WHEN MY FOCUS IS ON THE PEOPLE IN MY LIFE AND HOW I RELATE TO THEM. THIS ALLOWS ME TO.....

HUMOR and PLAYFULNESS

Being playful helps you find enjoyment in everyday life. While the modes change, play still helps adults integrate with one another in the same way that it does for children. Playful (and appropriate) behavior can open the mind and soul of human beings to relate more meaningfully to each other. Socially, it can simply be useful as an icebreaker. Being playful in our long-term relationships, like marriages, can often open the doors for intimacy that isn't available otherwise.

It is also important to note how beneficial humor is to us when we are going through difficult times. Laughter is the sudden release of built-up nervous tension and stress. That's why laughter feels so good! Research shows that laughter is very beneficial to our health. Being able to see a particular situation with a sense of humor and playfulness reminds us not to take ourselves too seriously.

Playfulness is connected to the child in us. Do not lose your ability to be playful. Playfulness is not something you outgrow, like clothing. The gauge of when to be playful is dictated by those around you and their comfort level with your playfulness, outgoing style and directness. Being playful is how we connect and bond with one other. Knowing how and when to use humor is a critical skill that feeds life into a relationship.

We want to reemphasize that your humor needs to be healthy and is never at the expense of others. When you choose to use humor in your relationships, make sure that the cues and behaviors of others indicate that your humor is appropriate and acceptable.

Humor is one of the most effective tools to discern the quality of a relationship. When there is laughter, the relationship is healthy. On the other hand, when the laughter stops, the relationship is on the down side. Here are some ways to make sure that laughter remains ever-present.

Humor changes how we feel, how we think, and how we behave. When we feel good, we reach out and connect with others. We are more open to trying new things, taking risks and being open to possibilities. In addition, humor improves our biochemistry! Studies indicate that people who practice humor

74

enjoy an increase in certain antibodies and a reduction in stress hormones, while depressed people experience a suppression of their immune system.

A sense of humor can go a long way toward helping you and your partner get through difficult times. When you lighten up, you take control of your troubles instead of allowing them to control you.

 I'm saddened to see adults so intense and serious that their ability to belly laugh or smile is forgotten. I am aware of how important laughter and playfulness are in my own relationships. I find that being able to play and laugh relieves my stress better than anything else I've come across.

 Our family, from the youngest to Grandpa, play games such as Monopoly and Yahtze. It brings out the child in us and the whole family has fun. We play games that include everyone so no one feels left out. Games bring out playful energy. Jeni and I bring playful energy to our business meetings. Our customers pick up on how relaxed we are and they relax as well. It helps to solidify our business relationships.

GAUGING YOUR HUMOR and PLAYFULNESS
Where do you measure up?

> **FAR LEFT (RED ZONE): YOU HAVE LITTLE OR NO HUMOR; LACKING PLAYFULNESS.**

- You are stern, serious, stuffy, guarded, inhibited, and restrained.
- You are unable to laugh at yourself or see the humor in situations.

> **THE MIDDLE (GREEN ZONE): YOU APPRECIATE HUMOR.**

- You are happy, lively, and able to joke with others.
- You are uninhibited; ready to take a few risks.
- You are learning to trust yourself.
  You are pleasant to be with and exhibit an appreciable amount of "spunk." This means that, from your behavior, no one would doubt that you are a lively and fun person to be with.

> **FAR RIGHT (RED ZONE): TOO MUCH OF A GOOD THING, YOU ARE TOO PLAYFUL.**

- You are overly playful, overly humorous; not being serious enough in serious situations.
- You laugh at the expense of others rather than with others.

CONSIDER THIS!

 Relationships are dances. Your playfulness is part of "letting go" and enjoying the moment with a partner. You are no longer caught up in the pressure to have all the right steps. This allows you to pay attention to your partner to see if he/she is having fun as well. Let's tie up a few lessons presented earlier in this book. I reference what Troy and Jeni learned about how much playfulness and acceptance made them better dancers together. They got more out of their dance lesson experience. In life relationships, being playful is an important lesson to bonding with a partner.

To get more out of life and "dance well" with others, you need to be able to be humorous and playful. Learn to laugh with yourself and with others. Learn how to stop taking things so seriously that you stop enjoying the moment. And lastly, remember who and what is important to you.

Stop taking yourself so seriously. When you take yourself too seriously, it clouds your ability to be open to change. The only thing that allowed me to become a better dancer with Jeni was to look at the dance lessons with humor and playfulness. I had to be able to laugh at myself and all the mistakes I was making on the way to becoming a better dancer.

IF I WERE LOOKING FOR PLACES TO INTEGRATE HUMOR AND PLAYFULNESS IN MY LIFE, I WOULD BEGIN WITH....

4 **HOPE and OPTIMISM**

What is your story? Are you the cookie that crumbles? When something happens to you, when things get difficult and coping with challenges becomes a stretch, are you the person who curls up in a fetal position mumbling, "Call me when it is over." "What am I going to do?" "Why do these things always happen to me?"

It is important to remember that by choosing hope, you are stronger, regardless of the outcome. Hope and optimism is a choice. When you choose to have hope, you also have the belief that a solution is inevitable. Hope is the whisper you hear that tells you, "Keep going. It's going to get better."

There are many different definitions of hope, depending on which theorist you follow. But there are several common themes in all the definitions. Hope usually involves some uncertainty of an outcome, typically concerns matters of importance and usually reflects a person's moral values. Hope is frequently considered a temporary condition that is specific to a given situation.

Hope is definitely not the same thing as optimism. It is not the conviction that something will turn out well, but the certainty that something makes sense, regardless of how it turns out.

I challenge clients daily regarding their beliefs about their learned helplessness. Many people become so programmed to view themselves as helpless and powerless that they continue to stay imprisoned and tethered to that negative belief structure. Optimism, however, is the belief that future events will have positive outcomes. Optimism has been linked to various aspects of psychological and physical well-being in adults and children. The beneficial effects of optimism and positive coping skills have been shown to enhance one's ability to deal with stress and depression. I believe that optimism is a choice.

I believe that optimism is always looking for the bright side of things. It may be hard to imagine, but there is a bright side to any situation. Choosing optimism can and must be learned. Hope is the fuel that keeps you always searching for the bright side.

GAUGING YOUR HOPE and OPTIMISM
Where do you measure up?

FAR LEFT (RED ZONE): YOU HAVE NO HOPE OR OPTIMISM.

- You are negative, dark, hopeless and desperate.
- You see life as an assembly line, replete with people who have zombie-like movements, all merely going through the motions.

THE MIDDLE (GREEN ZONE): YOU ALWAYS CHOOSE TO LOOK ON THE BRIGHT SIDE.

- You have a realistic sense of optimism.
- You look for something positive instead of searching for the negative.
- You start each day excited about the future.
- You are driven by optimism while keeping a hopeful eye on the future.

FAR RIGHT (RED ZONE): YOU HAVE TOO MUCH HOPE OR OPTIMISM.

- You are being rightly criticized for not being real or for being unrealistic. People might accuse you of this behavior by saying, "You always seem to have your head in the clouds."
- You are not prepared for consequences, especially when the future is uncertain.
- You do not combine hope with realism. You may want to be an Olympic contender but you do not have the ability.
- You hope for your wishes to happen, but your energies would be better directed if they were based in realism.

Our thoughts lead to feelings, which then lead to behaviors. You have a clear choice. You can choose to focus on thinking that things will get better, rather than worrying about what terrible "something" is lurking around the next corner. You can choose. What you allow yourself to think about or to focus on will absolutely affect how you move through each situation. The difference happens when you choose hope and then let that hope influence your life.

 Hope and optimism are like a light that you turn on to make things look even brighter. Shower the people in your life with hope and optimism and pepper your own thoughts with the same. People can pick up on your intentions. It's important to choose to operate with hope and optimism. Having hope means that, whatever you are dealing with, you maintain the belief, "things are going to be okay."

IF I WERE TO CHOOSE HOPE AND OPTIMISM, MY FOCUS THEN WOULD BE ON.....

 **SPIRITUALITY**

Spirituality is the dynamic web that connects us to God or a higher power as well as to one another. It creates a common bond comprised of compassion, empathy, forgiveness, gratitude, generosity, concern for others and love.

The search for meaning in our lives is the process that creates the foundation of our spirituality. It is inspired by our connection with ourselves, with others, and with our God. Spirituality fosters the development and use of our character strengths in all aspects of our life. Spirituality can help us operate from a place of purity, wholesomeness and authenticity.

Faith is the guidepost that helps us nurture and grow our spirituality. We define faith as having a loyalty to a person, God and/or a way of living. It is a firm belief or conviction without tangible proof arising from a decision to trust.

Faith allows us to focus on God. Faith makes us stronger as individuals because it allows us to choose to stand for something outside of ourselves versus falling for all the seductive temptations that life throws at us. Inspiration from God comes in the form of love, security and acceptance. When you are looking for inspiration, be assured that if it is of God, it will be an uplifting message. "God moments" are not about fear, anxiety or other self-depreciating thoughts, or about being self-absorbed. When you choose spirituality as an operating tool in your life, you choose to never be alone.

Granted, you can use these tools without having a sense of faith and still find a sense of happiness in relationships. However, we believe that you are more apt to have a stronger foundation and find life success if you choose to have faith.

 Spirituality is all about relationships. It encompasses my relationship with myself, with others, with my environment and with my God. My spirituality helps me remain centered and more connected in these relationships as my faith in God expands and grows.

 Spirituality is my reminder that there is more in life than just me. Spirituality is my connection to God that gives me a purpose and a plan for how I live my life each day. It reminds me to focus on others and share the joy of knowing

that I am not alone in this world. We all have a purpose, and it is always centered on others and not ourselves. Faith gives me the fuel to always focus on the needs of those around me.

GAUGING YOUR SPIRITUALITY
Where do you measure up?

FAR LEFT (RED ZONE): YOU LACK A SENSE OF SPIRITUALITY, PURPOSE AND FAITH.

- You feel separate and alone.
- You believe that when you die, you are gone. Dead.
- You feel you only have yourself to count on.

THE MIDDLE (GREEN ZONE): YOU HAVE A SENSE OF SPIRITUALITY, PURPOSE AND FAITH.

- You show respect, honoring or paying tribute to the idea that there is something greater than you that guides how life unfolds.
- You believe that you should be reaching out to assist the sick, the needy and the less fortunate.
- You know that your faith will bring you peace, joy and happiness.
- You have a sense of a greater being that provides life balance and keeps you centered on your pathway.

- Your faith relieves you of the responsibility of coping with life and taking responsibility for your choices and the situation you are in.
- You are living life by a rigid religious order or cult. You are not practicing logical, common sense or social awareness, nor seeing your surroundings for what they really are.
- You demand or insist that all of your beliefs must be adopted by all, and all must abide by your religious directives or doctrine.
- You expect to be rescued in troubled times. You are not willing to make an effort on your own behalf to save yourself.

CONSIDER THIS!

 Spirituality is the thread that ties us together as we rise above ourselves, seek meaning in our existence, and seek relationship with God. In these ways, spiritual seeking connects us and brings us closer together. You express your spirituality and your relationship with God through prayer, through your interactions with others and with nature. When you use this tool, your will find yourself inspiring and lifting up others. Spirituality is when you are coming from your spiritual convictions to connect with others and lift them up.

 Spirituality is like having a navigational compass that always points you in the right direction as you travel your life's path.

I EXPERIENCE A SENSE OF FAITH WHEN I.....

6 COURAGE

The root of the word courage is "cor" — the Latin word for "heart". In one of its earliest forms, the word courage had a very different definition than it does today. Courage originally meant, "to speak one's mind by telling all one's heart." Over time, this definition has changed. Today, courage is synonymous with being heroic. Heroics are appreciated and we certainly need heroes! Perhaps, we've lost touch with the idea that speaking honestly and openly about who we are, about what we're feeling, and about our experiences (positive or negative) can also be a definition of courage.

Courage is not something we are born with or that can be given to us. Courage is a desirable quality that we practice. We believe courage is the ability and willingness to confront whatever it is that prevents us from moving forward. Whether it is fear, pain, danger, uncertainty or intimidation, we use courage as a vehicle to move forward.

We can choose physical courage when we confront physical pain, hardship, death or the threat of death.

We can choose moral courage to stand up for what is right and ethical especially when presented with popular opposition, shame, scandal or discouragement.

The thought of choosing courage can be overwhelming at times. Our intention is to inspire people to look at every given moment to choose to be courageous. The variety of interactions that we have in all our relationships provides us with opportunities to choose courage every day. Making one courageous decision in the midst of fear is courage. We believe that those individual moments of choosing courage will grow exponentially over time and infiltrate all our relationships.

"Courage is not the absence of fear. It is acting in spite of it."~ Mark Twain

I believe courage is a quality that we can develop and model for our children. We do this when we openly and honestly choose to overcome the fears or obstacles that prevent us from moving forward or taking action. Courage drives our children to tell the truth even when they don't believe it's in their best interests. Courage keeps our children from writing off a friend who has taken a wrong turn in life. Courageous generosity motivates our children to give their allowance to a food bank instead of buying a new video game for their gaming system.

Courage is a huge theme in my life. It seems that I'm either praying for some courage or feeling grateful for having found a little bit of courage to move forward. Likewise, I'm appreciating it in other people. I don't think that makes me unique. Everyone wants to be brave.

T *I have experienced many situations which have required me to choose the character tool, courage, in order to move forward. Others face these same situations when they take responsibility for the safety and security of a spouse and children. Job changes along my career pathway and other tough decisions all taught me to choose courage in the face of fear. This gave me a chance for new opportunities rather than be stuck in a position I didn't like. Choosing courage in tough situations enabled me to reach for something new. I had enough faith and courage that I was able to apply my skill sets to new situations enabling me to adapt. I believe the sign of a courageous person is someone who feels fear, recognizes fear and still goes on to do what he or she believes is right.*

GAUGING YOUR COURAGE
Where do you measure up?

> **FAR LEFT (RED ZONE): YOU ARE NOT CHOOSING COURAGE.**

- Your decisions are solely emotion-based. Making decisions based on fear might be expressed as, "I'm not even going to try for the promotion because I might not get it" or "I'm not going to answer the question because I might be wrong and people will think I'm stupid."

- You fear rejection. Fear of rejection might sound like, "I won't ask so-and-so out on a date because she might not see me as being good enough" or "I am fearful to stand up for what is right because others might reject me."
- You allow your fear to paralyze you preventing you from making any decisions.
- You allow the negative "what ifs" to dominate your thoughts.

> **THE MIDDLE (GREEN ZONE): YOU CHOOSE COURAGE IN THE FACE OF FEAR.**

- You do the right thing in spite of feeling fear.
- You stand up for what is right and ethical.
- You feel fear yet choose to act.
- You persevere in the face of adversity.

> **FAR RIGHT (RED ZONE): YOU USE COURAGE IN AN UNHEALTHY WAY.**

- You do not use the element of fear when making decisions. Example: leaping into a dangerous situation without considering the consequences.
- You act courageous as a means of impressing someone. Example: "I'm going to walk the ledge of this building so everyone will think I'm courageous."
- You create crisis and chaos so you can play the role of the hero.

CONSIDER THIS!

It is my experience that people who choose to be courageous never regret their decision. People who choose to be motivated solely by fear always end up regretting their choice.

Choosing courage in the face of a difficult situation is the hardest part. It is easy to let the what-ifs and potential problems dampen your desire to be courageous. Once you make the choice to be courageous, you will be able to manage any situation that comes your way.

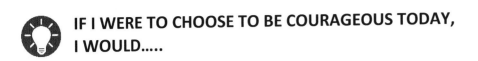

**IF I WERE TO CHOOSE TO BE COURAGEOUS TODAY,
I WOULD.....**

7 FORGIVENESS and MERCY

Forgiveness makes us stronger because we are essentially accepting something that we cannot change. We are mindfully choosing to be present versus focusing on the past.

Injustice and revenge are the two major reasons for not forgiving. When you think about things in your life where forgiveness was not possible, do you feel that life was not fair to you?

When injustice and revenge have been your focus, you might have wanted to "get even" or show the other person how hurt you were. At times, you may obsess over wanting revenge even though that desire to get even keeps you stuck and unable to move on in life. "I will move forward when you know how hurt I am."

Forgiveness is not forgetting. Forgiveness does not excuse someone for doing something unhealthy nor does it erase an unhealthy event or even validate it. When you forgive, it doesn't mean that you approve of what happened. Forgiveness is simply accepting and choosing not to focus on the past or getting even.

Forgiveness is what you do for yourself – what you give to you, not to other people. It means that you're giving yourself permission to move on with your life. Forgiveness allows you to move forward from a negative event, person or space in time. You can move forward in life and stop driving your car focusing on your rear view mirror. Face forward not backwards!

Forgiveness is a choice. Don't wait for it to suddenly wash over you.

Don't give away your power. The pain of what happened is inevitable, but continuing to suffer is optional. The only person you can control is you. By constantly reliving the pain of what happened, you give away your power to the person who wronged you.

Don't cling to negative feelings. Anger is often an outward sign of hurt, fear, guilt, grief or frustration. While the pain may never completely disappear, forgiveness can help you release the anger and bring those in your life closer to you.

There is no right timeline for forgiveness. For some people, making peace happens suddenly and spontaneously. For others, it takes time and a great deal of thought and effort. You may have to make a conscious effort every day to forgive, and actually say, "I'm letting this go. I'm not going to invest hatred, bitterness, anger, resentment in this person anymore. I am choosing to focus on what is in my life today." You can find closure in forgiveness.

You can't change the things that happened in your life, but you can decide how you interpret and respond to them.

E *I believe it is in our nature to want to right a wrong, especially when we've been ill-treated. We have a desperate need to make people who have wronged us understand how they have affected us. Some people are very comfortable staying in the victim role. They expend a lot of energy trying to convince everyone else how they were wronged or mistreated. I believe I can either fuel the past, which I can never change, or I can fuel the present, investing in my relationships, which I can change.*

T *I believe that revenge and injustice are the main culprits that perpetuate cycles of self-abuse and victimhood. When I hold those negative feelings inside, they prevent me from being who I really am and experiencing the love and joy that I hold in my heart.*

GAUGING YOUR FORGIVENESS and MERCY
Where do you measure up?

> **FAR LEFT (RED ZONE): YOU CHOOSE NOT TO FORGIVE.**

- You are condemning.
- You are resentful.
- You are judgmental.
- You are vindictive.

> **THE MIDDLE (GREEN ZONE): YOU MAKE THE CHOICE TO FORGIVE.**

- You choose to show mercy.
- You see yourself as accountable and responsible. When you see yourself in this light, you won't blame others for the way you are or for where you are in life.
- You do not cling to negative feelings.

> **FAR RIGHT (RED ZONE): YOU CHOOSE TO FORGIVE AT THE EXPENSE OF YOUR WELL-BEING.**

- Your forgiveness is at the cost of your own self-respect and self-advocacy.
- You find yourself remaining in unhealthy situations and relationships.
- You use forgiveness as a way of surviving and going on to your next unhealthy experience.

CONSIDER THIS!

 I am certain that we have all been both wronged and forgiven. The question is, will we forgive? Can we choose to be courageous in our forgiveness even if the other person doesn't know or doesn't do anything to merit our forgiveness? What choice will you make when the opportunity to forgive comes up again?

Forgiveness is not natural. It is a conscious decision to choose an uncommon reaction. It requires courage to choose to forgive someone. Many people believe that revenge and injustice require courage. I want you to know that an "eye for an eye" philosophy leaves everyone blind.

WHO IS THE MOST DIFFICULT PERSON IN MY LIFE FOR ME TO FORGIVE? WHO HAS THE MOST DIFFICULT TIME FORGIVING ME?

8 CRITICAL THINKING and OPEN-MINDEDNESS

Critical thinkers are both skeptical and open-minded. They value fair mindedness and respect evidence. Critical thinkers are driven by reasoning. They will look at different points of view and change position when reason leads them to do so. Critical thinkers choose to look at choices and compare those choices to arrive at a solution. Critical thinking is the opposite of "knee jerk" reactions.

Critical thinkers slow down their decision-making process thus minimizing the potential of impulsivity or a lack of objectivity. Critical thinkers will assess the reasons for and against doing something and then make their decision based on the basis of that fair assessment.

Critical thinkers are open-minded even with people they disagree with. They give them a fair hearing because their goal is the truth or the best action. A critical thinker's goal is not simply to confirm what they already believe.

Open-mindedness is the environment that you create that allows you to look at all the scenarios from a healthy point of view. Open-mindedness is the willingness to search actively for evidence against one's favored beliefs, plans or goals, and to weigh such evidence fairly when it is available.

E *Here is an example I use in my sessions. I tell the story of going to the eye doctor for an eye exam. I start the exam by telling the doctor that I believe I don't need glasses...that I see everything there is to see. I was hopeful that the eye test would prove me right. The doctor performed the eye test and then asked me where I wanted to purchase the glasses that I needed. I had convinced myself I saw everything but when I looked at the world through my new lenses, I saw all that I was missing. When I did not wear glasses, my brain made up for the deficit by creating a belief that I was seeing everything...even though I clearly was not. The brain is so efficient that it makes up for what is missing and convinces you that you see everything there is to see, even though you are missing a part of the picture. When are you choosing not to wear your glasses in your life? In other words, what is it that is difficult for you to look at in your relationships?*

I believe that applied critical thinking is essential for effective planning and problem-solving skills. Critical thinking also takes my own personal bias out of the decision-making process.

GAUGING YOUR CRITICAL THINKING and OPEN-MINDEDNESS
Where do you measure up?

FAR LEFT (RED ZONE): YOU CHOOSE NOT TO USE CRITICAL THINKING.

- You make decisions based solely on emotions which are inconsistent and unpredictable. This creates crisis and chaos.
- You make impulsive decisions motivated by guilt, shame and or fear.
- You think your way is the only way.

THE MIDDLE (GREEN ZONE): YOU HAVE A CONSISTENT PROCESS TO RELY ON FOR MAKING DECISIONS.

- You ask questions.
- You define the problem.
- You examine evidence.
- You analyze assumptions.
- You avoid oversimplification.
- You consider other interpretations.
- You rely on reason rather than on emotion.

- You are fearful of taking risks or making changes.
- You look at all the options but are fearful of taking action.
- Your analysis becomes the end-result, not the means to an end.

CONSIDER THIS!

Critical thinking is an intellectual tool that you choose to use when you are in a situation where you need to be mindful and thoughtful about the solutions you are generating. It is a tool designed to help you with your problem-solving skills.

Prepare a plan of action to tackle the challenge in front of you. Be ready with alternatives in case the first plan goes awry. When backed with proper planning and preparation, execution is a simple, straightforward process. Applied critical thinking skills are essential for all effective planning, problem-solving, and decision-making processes. Continuous practice improves your thinking speed and gives you the ability to think on your feet. The ultimate challenge is to train your brain to go beyond natural instinct to arrive at logical conclusions even when making instant decisions.

 WHAT SITUATION IN MY LIFE RIGHT NOW REQUIRES CRITICAL THINKING?

⑨ RELATIONSHIP AWARENESS
INFLUENCING and INSPIRING OTHERS

The quality of our life is equal to the quality of our relationships. We can improve the quality of our relationships by raising our awareness of the significance of those relationships. Our attentiveness allows us to be thoughtful and mindful to the degree we invest in those relationships. What we shine light on is what grows. The more aware we are of our relationships, the more those relationships strengthen and grow.

It is important to recognize that we do influence and hopefully, inspire others in our relationships. We influence people either in a positive or a negative way. One way to imagine how our influence can positively affect others is to see it as a bubbling spring that flows from us to others and beyond. When we do influence others in a positive way, this spring becomes a river of inspiration that is a positive force that will motivate people and lift them up. This speaks to the analogy that a high tide lifts all boats. The privilege of quietly watching our influence lift others up is one of the greatest rewards of inspiring others.

People, places and experiences that provide positive influence help us move closer to our desired goals. The result is that we can be better than we were yesterday. Can you recall a time when a positive change in your thinking was inspired by someone else that empowered you to move beyond what you initially anticipated?

Jim Rohn[5], author and business philosopher said, "We become the combined average of the five people we hang around most." The higher the concentration of time spent around quality people and similar elements, the higher the quality of output we will have to flow from ourselves to others. We can search out and surround ourselves with people who have already been where we want to go. We can be in places and engage in activities that keep us stretched slightly beyond our comfort zone with the understanding that stretching induces growth. And, we can contribute to the success of others by modeling a positive lifestyle.

---

[5] www.jimrohn.com/resource-library.html.

Life is a continual flow of learning and teaching, inputs and outputs. By being aware of the positive and negative elements in our environments, we will not only incorporate things into our lives that create better results, but we will also have a greater level of vision, belief, and expertise.

Try this formula for influencing and inspiring others:

> ### Challenge + Encourage + Motivate = INSPIRATION
>
> **CHALLENGE:** Create a demand to be, do and have greater than what presently exists.
>
> **ENCOURAGE:** Provide an external *"You can do this!"* in a way that it becomes the recipient's permanent internal *"I can do this!"*
>
> **MOTIVATE:** Instill a sense of purpose that becomes an impetus for achievement.

E *As a therapist, I am always conscious of the power of influence. I have learned that it is not a question of "if" we influence others; it is a question of "how." The destruction that results from negatively influencing the people and relationships around us is devastating. I have seen the detrimental consequences ripple through generations. It often becomes a legacy in a family system.*

And so, I am very aware of the power of my influence during a therapy session with a client. It is critical for my clients as well as all my relationships that I try to motivate people in a positive way. Inspiring others with genuine encouragement allows me to connect with people on a spiritual level and it is always positive. It always lifts people up...including me!

 I've learned that people feed on what I project. Just as people feed on messages sent by my words and actions, they are also influenced by my words and actions. If I am negative or pessimistic about a situation, others will sense what I feel. Thus, my emotions might be as contagious as a bad cold. Even when I am not influenced by character strengths, I still have an influence on others. I've learned I need to be careful about what messages I send, as those messages are

more lasting than I can imagine. When I am aware of my words and actions, I become more aware of how I influence and inspire others.

GAUGING YOUR RELATIONSHIP AWARENESS
Where do you measure up?

FAR LEFT (RED ZONE): YOU ARE NOT AWARE OF AND DO NOT FOCUS ON YOUR RELATIONSHIPS.

- You are negatively influencing others.
- You are not aware of or sensitive to how your words and actions are affecting those around you.

THE MIDDLE (GREEN ZONE): YOU RECOGNIZE AND EXERCISE YOUR ABILITY TO INFLUENCE YOUR RELATIONSHIPS IN A POSITIVE MANNER.

- You are very diligent in making sure that you are investing daily in your relationships in a positive manner.
- You are motivated to influence others in an inspirational way and your words and actions support this.

FAR RIGHT (RED ZONE): YOU ARE USING YOUR INFLUENCE AND AWARENESS OF YOUR RELATIONSHIPS TO IMPACT PEOPLE IN AN UNHEALTHY WAY.

- You influence people to echo your thoughts, emotions and perceptions.
- You use influence to manipulate people to get what you want.
- You lift yourself up at the expense of others.

CONSIDER THIS!

 Healthy communication is the vehicle to inspire others. You can't influence or inspire unless you can effectively communicate what your vision or goal is and how you plan to achieve it. Inspiration dances with trust. Trust only comes when others share their views with you and believe that you respect their ideas. You must listen as well as speak. Healthy communication is key to strengthening your relationship awareness. Relationship awareness is directly linked with the satisfaction and peace that you desire to feel at the end of the day. The more you invest in your relationships in a positive way, the better the quality of your relationships will be. If you are not investing in your relationships, what are you investing in?

 You are going to have an impact on people. It is not a question of "if" you are going to have an impact on them, it is a question of "how" you are going to influence them. The more character tools that you learn and apply to your relationships and your life, the more confidence you will have that you are influencing people in a positive way.

HOW CAN I USE MY INFLUENCE IN A POSITIVE MANNER TO INSPIRE THE PEOPLE IN MY RELATIONSHIPS?

10 STRIVING FOR EXCELLENCE

Striving for excellence is the attitude and/or process of choosing to do your best at everything you do. Striving for excellence is about knowing yourself and your strengths. It is about realizing and accepting responsibility for the roles and influences that you have on the lives of those around you. This encompasses all your relationships –family, business, social and community.

Many people confuse striving for excellence with striving for perfection. Striving to be perfect is a method of sabotaging our success. Being perfect has no finish line and is unachievable. Striving for excellence is the key to living a super-charged life. Striving implies that we must keep practicing, keep at it and not give up despite failed attempts.

If you want to get the most out of life in every way, then you have to put the most into it. It sounds like a cliché but it is absolutely true – you get out of life what you put into it. We have to put our best foot forward in every endeavor.

When you choose to strive for excellence, you surround yourself with passionate people. You build a network of passionate positive people and frequently spend time with them. People of like minds inspire and support each other. When you choose to strive for excellence, you pour your heart and mind into your activities. You are open to new ideas and adopt an attitude to continually seek ideas for self-improvement. You ask yourself at the end of the day, "Did I give the very best of myself to those around me?"

 "The quality of a person's life is in direct proportion to their commitment to excellence, regardless of their chosen field of endeavor." This quote by the famous football coach, Vince Lombardi, reminds me that anyone, regardless of their chosen profession or job, can improve the quality of their life with a commitment to excellence.
I can choose this attitude anytime and it is not connected to any particular outcome. Each time I choose to use this tool, I directly impact my relationships and my life in a positive way.

 If you're not growing, you're dying. If you're not working for good, you're working for bad. I think of these choices every day as I remind myself of my responsibilities to the people around me. I have found that striving for

excellence in all areas of my life is the fuel that drives me to be the best I can be. I know that my measuring stick is that I try to do everything a little bit better today than I did yesterday. Why would I want to do anything else? My family, friends and customers expect and deserve nothing less.

GAUGING YOUR STRIVE FOR EXCELLENCE
Where do you measure up?

FAR LEFT (RED ZONE): YOU CHOOSE NOT TO STRIVE FOR EXCELLENCE IN ANY PART OF YOUR LIFE.

- You are fearful of change.
- You are content to not improve your performance or relationships.
- Your focus is on the obstacles, difficulties and problems of the task at hand.
- You give up in the face of obstacles and present yourself as having no responsibility in the outcome.

THE MIDDLE (GREEN ZONE): YOU CHOOSE TO STRIVE FOR EXCELLENCE IN ALL PARTS OF YOUR LIFE.

- You make an agreement with yourself to do the best you can in all areas of your life.
- You establish goals to push you beyond what you believe you are capable of doing.

- Your drive for excellence is at the cost of other areas in your life... most especially your relationships.
- You strive for financial goals that come at the expense of shortchanging your relationships.
- Your drive in one area can leave you lacking in other life areas. For example, I am striving to be a great golfer and it comes at the expense of my job and my relationships.

CONSIDER THIS!

Striving for excellence implies that we must keep practicing and not give up despite failed attempts. I believe we must strive for excellence – doing all things in the best possible manner. We do not tolerate or accept second grade, shoddy work in others; hence, we too must be putting our best into the job at hand. Enjoy the work, be enthusiastic with the results, and cheer the people who do excellent work! Conversely, we do not strive for perfection, because it is an impossible state to achieve! In trying to do so, we may become tyrannical, shouting and screaming orders, pushing people to extremes, and become a very unattractive person. Perfection kills the joy of doing any work. Hence, "Strive for excellence, not perfection!"

To me, striving for excellence means changing what you can and not worrying about that which you cannot change. When you stop worrying and putting energy towards the things you cannot change, you will realize how much more energy you do have to devote towards the things you can change.

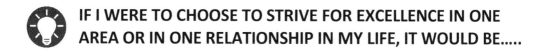

IF I WERE TO CHOOSE TO STRIVE FOR EXCELLENCE IN ONE AREA OR IN ONE RELATIONSHIP IN MY LIFE, IT WOULD BE.....

SELF-REGULATION and SELF-MANAGEMENT

Self-control separates us from our ancient ancestors and the rest of the animal kingdom, thanks to our large prefrontal cortices. Rather than respond to immediate impulses, we can plan and evaluate alternative actions and refrain from doing things we will regret. We can also take advantage of these innately human abilities by developing wisdom and willpower.

The importance of developing self-control during our preschool age years is illustrated by a classic longitudinal study conducted at Stanford University in the 1960's by Michael Mischel. The researcher presented two options to hungry four-year-old children. They could have one marshmallow right away or get two marshmallows fifteen minutes later when the researcher returned after running an errand. One third of the children opted for one marshmallow. Years later, a follow-up study was administered when the same participants graduated from high school. Mischel found that the children who waited (for the second marshmallow) now possessed the habits of successful people (Beachman, 2009). They were positive, self-motivated, and persistent in their pursuit of goals (Beachman, 2009). These habits point to successful marriages, higher incomes, and better health. The study also showed that the participants who did not wait earned lower SAT scores, were indecisive, less confident, and stubborn; all predictors of unstable marriages, low incomes, and poor health (Beachman, 2009).

A similar and more recent longitudinal study showed that preschoolers who exhibited high levels of delay-of-gratification, later displayed greater cognitive control than teens who had exhibited lower levels of delay-of-gratification during preschool (Eigsti, Zayas, Mischel, Shoda, Ayduk, Dadlani, Davidson, Aber, and Casey, 2006). Self-control develops when children begin to differentiate between short-term and long-term outcomes. When they realize that a long-term outcome is greater, they choose to delay gratification in their best interest. Researchers have found that the ability to choose delayed rewards increases with age and levels off in the early 30's. The capacity to choose a future reward is a function of the prefrontal lobes of the brain. Such capacity demands, "a special kind of memory in which information about the past and the future can be held in mind, while carrying out the responses needed to accomplish the goal" (Barkley, 2007, p. 52).

Self-management begins with self-awareness. Self-awareness speaks to our ability to be aware of what we are thinking and feeling. Once we become aware of what we are thinking and feeling, we can choose how to manage those thoughts and feelings in a mindful, appropriate and healthy manner. The idea here is to either choose to manage our thoughts and feelings or we choose to allow our thoughts and feelings to manage us.

Familiarizing yourself with your thoughts, emotions, what influences you and how things impact you, allows you to strengthen your self-management and self-control.

When you know yourself better, you're inclined to be a better decision maker. You will be better at making decisions as you know how those decisions will affect you and those around you.

This tool may be more valuable to you than relying solely on your intellect. Becoming aware of what you are thinking and feeling and then choosing what you want to do with those thoughts and feelings can be an essential asset to you. Your self-awareness and self-management skills allow you to connect and interact with people in an authentic and genuine way. When you are aware of what you are thinking and feeling you are less driven by my thoughts and feelings.

This allows you to be present in your interactions with people by focusing on the other person and becoming aware of their needs and feelings, rather than focusing only on what you are thinking and feeling.

 I believe that when you practice self-control, self-regulation and self-management, you realize that your words and actions have power. It is important to not always be the person who speaks up right away with the answer or the one who likes to impress others with their knowledge.

 Before I act, I go through possible scenarios in my mind as to how each word and action will affect those around me. This allows me to see the potential positive and/or negative consequences that may play out because of my actions and/or words. I am convinced that this is a good filter to run everything through before speaking or acting.

GAUGING YOUR SELF-CONTROL
Where do you measure up?

FAR LEFT (RED ZONE): YOU LACK SELF-CONTROL.

- You say whatever comes into your head without consideration or respect for others.
- You do what you want simply because it is what you want.
- You are impulsive. You lack an emotional filter which prevents you from saying certain things out loud.
- You have little self-control over your behavior. You blame others for your negative behavior using it as an excuse for not taking responsibility for your own actions.

THE MIDDLE (GREEN ZONE): YOU OPERATE FROM THE "SWEET SPOT" – THE BALANCE BETWEEN SELF-MANAGEMENT AND SELF-REGULATION.

- You are thoughtful about what you do.
- You weigh the consequences of all your actions.
- You have control over your decisions so you know they are appropriate and healthy.
- You know that you are 100% responsible for what you say and do.
- You are appropriately spontaneous.

FAR RIGHT (RED ZONE): YOU EXHIBIT TOO MUCH SELF-CONTROL AND REGULATION.

- You fear making decisions. Thus, decisions are not made.
- You are driven by such rigid self-control that you cannot allow

yourself to be playful, fun and vulnerable.

- You have no spontaneity.

CONSIDER THIS!

 Self-management speaks to your ability to think and feel anything. It allows you to take a deep breath or a pause to decide if you need to act on every thought and feeling that is going through your head. It is your ability in the midst of conflict with your spouse, your children or your colleagues to choose whether you want to "be right" or to "be happy" in that particular situation.

This tool activates a process within you that encompasses more than self-management. This process allows you to separate your thoughts and feelings from who you authentically are. Self-management means that you get to manage yourself instead of being managed by the environment or things outside of yourself.

You will find many opportunities to use the tool, "Self-control, Self-regulation and Self-management". You will be faced with hundreds of opportunities every day to use this tool. By choosing to use this tool you will avoid crises and chaos as your choices will be more consistent and predictable.

I WOULD BENEFIT FROM CHOOSING MORE SELF-CONTROL, SELF-REGULATION AND SELF-MANAGEMENT IN THESE AREAS OF MY LIFE.....

(12) ZEST, ENTHUSIASM AND ENERGY

Zest is defined as having a sense of enthusiasm, energy, excitement and liveliness. When you lend your enthusiasm or energy to others and then spice it up with zest, you give "life" to relationships. In essence, you give "life" to whatever you do, and you'll feel more alive in the process.

You can rise from bed in the morning like a zombie, unconscious but going through the motions to grab your cup of coffee, or you can start the day with a conscious choice for zest that sets the tone for the rest of your day. You can decide to give 100% of your attention to your family by focusing on them and not yourself. Imagine how everyone might feel if you and your family began their day with a positive outlook! Which appeals to you more?

We believe that choosing zest means living your life with a sense of excitement and energy, and anticipation for the future. It is seeing life as an adventure in which you are an active participant.

- When you have zest, you exude excitement and energy while approaching tasks in life. It is important to perform all of your tasks wholeheartedly while also being adventurous, vivacious and energetic.
- The character tools Zest and Courage (Tool # 6) go hand in hand. Each fuels the other when completing challenging situations and tasks.
- People with zest simply enjoy things more.
- Zest is a positive attitude that reflects a person's approach to life with anticipation, energy, enthusiasm and excitement.

 I believe that when I choose zest it is absolutely contagious. It is contagious in my relationships with my daughters, my wife, my neighbors, my clients, my family and friends. If I am going to give somebody something, why not give them something to lift them up...zest!

I associate zest with my rule of giving 100%. I believe that this rule offers the premise that whatever you do at work or at home, you promise yourself to always set your standard of behavior at 100% performance. If you give any less than that, you are shortchanging everyone, including yourself. You don't want to do that. You're worth more than that. You can trust that there are already enough people out there who do shortchange themselves.

I believe that this rule is the reason for my success in business, relationships and life. At the start of every day, I set my performance barometer at 100%... my gold standard of performance. This promise includes moments I spend with my wife, children, friends and any others.

This 100% Rule has been my "secret weapon" in business, helping me win and maintain business I never thought possible. It has helped me weather economic storms, keeping my business more level than static, in spite of economic ups and downs.

At the end of each business day, my wife, Jeni, and I ask one another if each has been able to maintain the 100% Rule. If there is an area in which one of us has fallen short, it goes to the top of the "to do" list for the next business day. Giving as much as possible may at times be too much to expect from one another. However, that's what I feel is my best challenge and keeps reminding me to "give all I can" every day.

GAUGING YOUR ZEST, ENTHUSIASM and ENERGY
Where do you measure up?

- You are always feeling tired.
- You feel a debilitating sadness.
- You have a pessimistic attitude.
- You are low on energy.
- You are ineffective with others.
- You are unlikely to push yourself.

THE MIDDLE (GREEN ZONE): YOU ARE MOTIVATED WITH ZEST, ENTHUSIASM AND ENERGY.

- You are excited, confident, motivated and active.
- You relish the challenges of life.
- Your zest is internally driven.

FAR RIGHT (RED ZONE): YOUR ZEST IS OVER THE TOP AND TOO MUCH OF A GOOD THING.

- You do not appear real to others.
- You are difficult to relate to.
- You lack a genuine affect.
- You try to create the false impression of being a high-energy mover and shaker.
- You present yourself as a power person to be reckoned with, but you are not feeling it. Your appearance is fake.
- You abandon critical thinking in favor of feeling enthusiastic.

CONSIDER THIS!

 When you choose to use the tool, Zest, you are choosing to have excitement, motivation, creativity and inspiration in your life.

 The bottom line with this tool is to keep it real. Be authentic. Do give 100% of what you have and remember that zest must dance with authenticity. Giving 100% means approaching every day with excitement and energy. It's common sense that if you decide you are too tired to give 100% and can give only 60%, you can be sure you will get 60% back. Is that good enough for you? Or would

you want someone to give you 100% of his or her attention? Once you become used to 100%, it is hard to accept less.

 **WHAT AREAS IN MY LIFE ARE LACKING ZEST, ENTHUSIASM AND ENERGY?**

⑬ KINDNESS and GENEROSITY

Kindness is a character tool from which the other character tools flow. It is a simple yet profound virtue with a far-reaching impact. Warm memories are frequently associated with small yet powerful acts of kindness. Our personal and professional relationships change and grow by the caring and compassionate action of others. Being kind means placing the needs of others above your own for the betterment of everyone involved.

Generosity involves giving from the heart without a price tag. Being generous means giving without the expectation of receiving anything in return.

Kindness and generosity are motivated by a care and concern for others. By definition, they are devoid of the assurance of reciprocity, a gain in reputation or other self-benefit.

Acts of kindness reshape our self-image, promote healthy and strong relationships and cultivate peace, contentment and satisfaction in our lives. Scientific research clearly demonstrates that providing an act of kindness boosts not only our immune system but also our production of serotonin. It is amazing that not only does the person providing the act of kindness benefit from increased serotonin levels but so do the people receiving that act of kindness. What is even more amazing is that people simply observing this act of kindness benefit as well!

Take a moment to recall when someone extended kindness or generosity to you. Now recall a time when you witnessed an act of kindness or generosity. Finally, recall a time when you extended an act of kindness or generosity toward others. How did these acts of kindness affect you? We hope that an act of kindness and generosity, whether given, received or observed, has inexplicably warmed your heart!

 I must share a heart-warming experience I enjoyed both as a parent and as a human being. When my daughter, Emma, was in grade school, there was a boy in her class (Timmy) who was quite overweight. As you might expect he was the target of many jokes and was treated very badly by other kids (and even by some of the teachers). Timmy gave the impression that he was not a nice guy, mostly because of the fact that he was constantly being picked on.

One day, Emma came home from school upset because Timmy was getting picked on so much. She also mentioned that he had no school supplies because his family could not afford them. He was constantly asking to borrow paper, which just gave the kids in his class even more reason to pick on him. That evening we discussed the situation in greater detail. Together we devised a plan for Emma to engage Timmy in a conversation and ask him what supplies he needed.

The next day Emma spent some time with Timmy and really came to realize that this young man had a heart of gold but rarely was able to show it because he was always on the defensive. Emma asked him if he would make a list of the supplies he needed. She told Timmy she would bring extra supplies that she had at home to school for him. Timmy put together a small list of three-ring binders, paper, pens, pencils and a pencil sharpener. Emma promised Timmy that she would help and he was most appreciative. That evening, Emma and I made a pilgrimage to the store where we bought everything on his list and then some! Emma remembered that Timmy also needed a new pencil box because the one he had was destroyed when one of the pens exploded. We added that to the list, as well as a backpack to carry all the supplies.

The next day, I brought the bag to the school and explained the situation to the principal. I asked the principal to give the bag to Timmy discreetly so that he would not feel embarrassed.

Later that day I picked up Emma after school and she was all smiles. She said the principal called Timmy down to his office and gave him the backpack. Timmy read the little note that Emma put inside saying that she hoped he had everything that he needed now and to enjoy the supplies. As Timmy walked into the classroom, he smiled at Emma and later thanked her very much for all the stuff. He loved it all! Emma said it was so cute to see him take out his new pencil box and to start arranging his pencils and pens. He seemed very happy.

That was a great experience for my daughter but I cannot tell you the joy it brought to me to see a young person acting upon something that was truly upsetting to her. Blossoming kindness and the willingness to take action are wonderful things to see. I encourage all the youth of this world to keep their hearts open and never be afraid to show random acts of kindness to those in need. No matter what your friends say, act upon what is in your heart. You never know what might happen – it may create a ripple effect for others to do the same! As for Timmy...I saw him walking home one day with his new back pack. It was a good feeling to know we had made a difference in his life!

I believe that when I choose to be kind and generous to my wife, my children, my customers and employees, I feel more connected with them. For example, I feel uplifted when I spend more time listening to a problem my customer may have at that moment, than I do focusing on business. The business will be taken care of at some point. However, the time I spend listening to that person about the problem they may have is priceless. Just being there to listen creates a bond that is invaluable in my relationship with that customer.

GAUGING YOUR KINDNESS and GENEROSITY
Where do you measure up?

FAR LEFT (RED ZONE): YOU ARE NOT SENSITIVE TO OTHERS NEEDS.

- You are only focused on your own needs.
- You are stingy and self-centered.
- You are apathetic.
- You exhibit a lack of caring.
- You have a mean attitude.

THE MIDDLE (GREEN ZONE): YOU ARE KIND AND GENEROUS.

- You extend kindness and generosity without any expectations.
- You serve and give to others without any expectations.

FAR RIGHT (RED ZONE): YOU USE KINDNESS IN A MANIPULATIVE AND SELF-SERVING MANNER.

- You use kindness and generosity to manipulate others for self-centered and self-serving purposes.
- Your kindness is at the expense of someone else.
- Your kindness is at the expense of you and/or your family.

CONSIDER THIS!

 Why be kind and generous? Because acts of kindness promote happiness and well-being! I believe that to be good at anything —including using the tool kindness and generosity —you have to practice it. Practice, in this case, means that each day you challenge yourself to look for opportunities to extend kindness and generosity without any strings attached.

 When you assume an attitude of service, you can do so with kindness and generosity. It doesn't matter if you extend kindness and generosity to a spouse, a friend, a business contact or a neighbor, you are still giving of yourself. As a result, you will enjoy the feeling of happiness you receive in return.

IF I WERE TO BE KIND AND GENEROUS TODAY, I WOULD CHOOSE TO.....

14 **HONESTY**

AUTHENTICITY and GENUINENESS

When you choose to be honest, you present yourself in a genuine and authentic manner. You are transparent with your motivations, intentions and commitments. You are accountable and responsible for your emotions and behaviors.

Choosing to be honest is a choice we can make not only through our words but through our behaviors as well. It is important that our words and our behaviors match up consistently. When your words and behaviors are in alignment, you are living your life in a genuine and authentic way.

Do you feel your image and the "real you" don't match up? Are you concerned? Do you worry there might be a gap between what people see in you and who you really are? Are you two different personas?

FRONT STAGE/BACK STAGE

Does your image and the "real you" match up? Is there a gap between what people see in you and who you really are?

Front Stage is the term we use to describe how others see you. It's how you perform. It's what you want people to know about you.

Back Stage is the term we use to describe who you truly are.

Does your Front Stage match your Back Stage?

Are you honest with your words and behaviors?

If you are a parent, do you discipline and guide your children in a way that keeps you humble and true to your beliefs? Do you speak and relate to your children in a way that is genuine and caring?

Are you real with the role in life that you play?

Are you doing the best you can to be real in your role as a spouse, a friend, a co-worker, a parent or an employee?

When you choose to be dishonest, you are choosing to be deceptive. It takes deception to cover deception. It is a race without a finish line. Deception comes at the cost of being in the present. If your focus is on what you need to say in order to feel or look good or if you focus on how you will respond to what people might say to you, then you have just taken a detour from authenticity.

When you choose to use character strengths like honesty and genuineness to be your authentic self, you will feel motivated and energized!

Are you strong enough to be your most authentic self?

E *For me, this tool has a 100% guarantee. Choosing to be authentic requires that I make a diligent effort to make sure that my front stage matches up with my back stage. It requires me to be honest with myself about who I am and how I want to present myself. When my front stage and my back stage are in alignment, I am authentic. When I interact with people from this level of authenticity, my level of genuineness is clear to other people. I know that each time I choose not to use this tool, I will regret my choice 100% of the time.*

T *This tool is what allows me to have a good night's sleep every night. I know that when I am honest and genuine with my actions during each day, I have presented myself as I really am and I don't have to worry about how people see me. I keep this tool in mind in all my actions and decision-making processes each day. My customers, friends and family know who I am and that they can rely on me being authentic today, tomorrow and each day in the future. It gives them confidence that they can always count on me.*

GAUGING YOUR HONESTY
Where do you measure up?

FAR LEFT (RED ZONE): YOU LACK HONESTY.

- You are driven by fear that you are not good enough, so you pretend to be what you are not.
- You have to cover up lies with other lies.
- You are deceptive.
- You are not authentic.

THE MIDDLE (GREEN ZONE): YOU ARE NATURAL AND 100% REAL.

- Your front stage matches your back stage.
- Your words and behaviors match up consistently.
- You are transparent with your motivations, intentions and commitments.

FAR RIGHT (RED ZONE): YOU ARE MANIPULATIVE AND SELF-FOCUSED.

- You use the appearance of being genuine to control others.
- Your honesty is at the cost of kindness and respect to others.
- You use honesty as a way to manipulate a situation or a person.

CONSIDER THIS!

My job as a therapist offers me the opportunity to see thousands of people. I am profoundly impacted every day by how toxic and cancerous deception can be in our relationships and our lives.   Deception presents itself in every session in some form whether it is an individual, a couple or a family. People believe it is easier to be deceptive than it is to risk being honest and showing their true authentic self. We have morphed into a culture that believes and accepts that it is easier to be deceptive than it is to be honest.

However, I can tell you that from my experience, people do crave authenticity and honesty, both within themselves as well as in their relationships.   I want to inspire you to take the risk to use this tool today. It is the one tool that will give you instant results both internally and externally. You will find that authenticity is contagious in your relationships.

Strive for the green zone.   Being who you really are is a challenge in today's society.   Everyone thinks they need to be someone else.   The grass is always greener on the other side.   I guarantee that if you choose to use this tool in all aspects of your life, you will immediately find the peace, satisfaction and contentment you seek.

LIST THREE CHARACTERTISTICS OF MY FRONT STAGE SELF:

LIST THREE CHARACTERTISTICS OF MY BACK STAGE SELF:

15 PERSEVERANCE

INDUSTRY and DILIGENCE

Perseverance means you finish what you start. You are industrious and prepared to take on difficult projects and follow through to completion. Perseverance requires drive, energy and action.

> **DRIVE + ENERGY + ACTION = PERSEVERANCE**
>
> Dedication
> Determination
> Endurance
> Persistence
> Stamina
> Steadfastness
> Tenacity

In our culture, we have a big problem with patience and perseverance. We expect instant results. When we are hungry, we want food…fast. Hence, fast food. When we are feeling uncomfortable, we look for an immediate way to feel better. We call this "instant gratification."

Perseverance is the direct opposite of instant gratification. Perseverance requires us to stay focused. When we choose perseverance, we choose to move forward despite the obstacles or the discomfort that often side-track us.

Many of the obstacles we experience in our lives revolve around relationships. Instant gratification gives us permission to walk away or deny that there are conflicts/obstacles in our relationships. We believe that when there is a problem, it is easier to walk away than to confront and push through the issues. We are only concerned about what is going to make us feel good right now. As we walk away from confrontations, we often find ourselves walking toward drugs, alcohol, pornography, gambling, etc.

Our relationships are never absent of times where we want to give up, turn our back or walk away. These are the times when perseverance will get you through any tough situation. Our relationships are worth fighting for! It is too easy to turn our backs and look for the easy fix instead of pushing forward and investing in a resolution. Perseverance is the answer when we feel like giving up.

When people are admired for their "survivor" skills, it's because of their ability to keep moving forward in life, in spite of obstacles in the way. They keep pace, one foot in front of the other, staying in motion in spite of circumstances that would make many individuals freeze in place.

What do you do when life throws you a curve? Do you have the energy and drive to keep on living or do you stop short in your tracks? Do you curl up in the fetal position, wanting someone to wake you when the problem is over? Do you hope someone will care enough to "rescue" you by telling you what to do or step in to help you until you get on your feet again?

When you choose to persevere, you are choosing to focus on the here and now because you can only persevere in that moment. Your life becomes satisfying and more peaceful than it would have been if you had allowed yourself to "cave in" during the crisis. It's a good idea to be mindful of what we teach our children. It's important to show them how to keep going in spite of a problem. When you persevere, you keep things going in spite of what may stand in your way.

 In my personal life, I view my relationships like a cage fight. Cage fights are interesting because no one is allowed to leave until the fight is over. There are no exits. Fighters must draw deep within themselves because they know there are no other options except for resolution. My marriage, my relationships with my children, my relationships with my family and friends have no exits.

One of my favorite quotes about perseverance is..."If I had to select one quality, one personal characteristic that I regard as being most highly correlated with success, whatever the field, I would pick the trait of persistence. Determination. The will to endure to the end, to get knocked down seventy times and get up off the floor saying. "Here comes number seventy-one!" (Richard M. Devos, co-founder Amway)

 I believe that success in life is very simple. It is never quitting or giving up. It is simply showing up each day and doing the best job I can at living up to my

responsibilities. Doing this leaves me satisfied and content that I am doing what I am supposed to be doing. I believe everything in our lives moves us towards something greater.

GAUGING YOUR PERSEVERENCE
Where do you measure up?

FAR LEFT (RED ZONE): YOU QUIT. YOU GIVE UP.

- You choose to not finish or complete difficult tasks.
- You procrastinate, getting less done.
- You're in the fetal position, seeing yourself as helpless and powerless.
- You deny or do not resolve conflicts in your relationships.

THE MIDDLE (GREEN ZONE): YOU PERSEVERE.

- You work until the job is done.
- You take pride in completing tasks.
- You focus on a specific task and stay directed.
- You push through conflicts in your relationships by using healthy confrontation.

FAR RIGHT (RED ZONE): YOU PERSEVERE IN AN UNHEALTHY MANNER.

- You persevere at an unhealthy cost to yourself.
- You persevere at the cost of someone else.
- You persevere for self-serving purposes.

CONSIDER THIS!

 Perseverance seems like a harder tool to introduce to people. People are programmed by our culture to seek out anything that is going to make us feel better right now. We are smothered by a variety of ways to gain instant gratification. The idea to delay pleasure or to push through discomfort is difficult for people to wrap their heads around.

Perseverance is one of the most important character tools that you can have in your tool kit. Perseverance is the fuel that will drive you to get better at using all the other tools. Perseverance does not necessarily mean that you will have successful completion of a task. It does mean that you will continue to move forward towards resolution.

Perseverance is the character tool where you choose to focus on the present and move forward... rather than being motivated and influenced by whatever your limiting emotion is at that moment.

 **THREE AREAS IN MY LIFE WHERE I CAN BENEFIT FROM USING THE CHARACTER TOOL, PERSEVERANCE, ARE.....**

16 UNCONDITIONAL LOVE

Our ability to choose to love unconditionally is the character tool that ties all of us together regardless of our religion, ethnic or socio-economic group. Do the people you love know how much you love them? Do you allow the people in your life to love you?

Love expresses itself in four different ways in a relationship. One expression of love is from the individual who is our primary source of affection, protection and care. A second form of love is for the individual we depend on for safety and security. The third form of love is the love that involves our passionate desire for emotional, physical, or sexual intimacy with an individual. The fourth expression of love is the love that we give and receive to people that we encounter and interact with in our lives.

The goal for all these expressions of love is that we love unconditionally…no strings attached!

Love fuels passion, hope and desire. It generates creativity and gives us purpose, making us feel alive. When we think of love, we typically think of romantic love, yet love can be expressed in a variety of ways –all unique, fulfilling and enriching our lives.

We all want to feel loved. We think about it, hope for it, fantasize about it, go to great lengths to achieve it, and believe that our lives are incomplete without it. The lack of unconditional love in our lives is the cause of most of our anger and confusion. It is no exaggeration to say that our emotional need for unconditional love is just as great as our physical need for air and food.

We cannot experience unconditional love until we first choose to love people unconditionally. Unconditional love is choosing to love without any strings attached.

Choosing to love unconditionally fills us with happiness and makes us feel whole!

E As a marriage and family therapist, I have found that relationships can involve more than one kind of love. They can start as one expression of love, and evolve into another over time. It is up to us to recognize and act upon the different kinds of love in our life. We cultivate this unique love and promote emotional well-being through our connections with our family members, friends, neighbors, and even pets!

T I believe that the capacity to love and to be loved is easily transferrable into the work place. Imagine what the work world might look like if more people demonstrated the capacity to love and be loved. Employees would feel truly appreciated rather than feeling taken for granted. Employees would feel more connected to each other rather than isolated from each other. And, employees might view each other as friends rather than competitors or enemies. I apply all these principles in my family business and it gives us a closer relationship with our customers, which in turn makes us more successful.

GAUGING YOUR UNCONDITIONAL LOVE
Where do you measure up?

> **FAR LEFT (RED ZONE): YOU CHOOSE NOT TO LOVE OR BE LOVED.**

- You believe you are "damaged goods" without the capacity to love or to be loved.
- You believe you are "empty" and cannot give or receive love.
- You believe you are permanently "broken" and "damaged" by your life experiences.
- You believe you are alone, isolated and cannot give what you do not have.
- You easily withhold love and end relationships when your

expectations are not met.

> **THE MIDDLE (GREEN ZONE): YOU VALUE CLOSE RELATIONSHIPS AND CONNECTIONS WITH OTHERS.**

- You express love without the expectation of getting anything in return.
- You choose to demonstrate love.
- You allow the people in your life to love you.
- You communicate to the people in your life how much you love them.
- You accept expressions of love from those around you at face value.

> **FAR RIGHT (RED ZONE): YOU CHOOSE NOT TO LOVE UNCONDITIONALLY.**

- You manipulate others with your love and your need for love comes at an unhealthy cost to others.
- You accept being in an unhealthy relationship without regard to the effect it has on everyone else in the family.
- You trade physical or emotional abuse for love.

CONSIDER THIS!

 Love begins with YOU! It is hard to feel worthy of love if someone is criticizing you all the time; especially, if that someone is your inner voice talking in your head. Stop comparing yourself to others and feeling like you are helpless and powerless.

It is important that you open up your eyes and see the variety of ways that people communicate their love to you. When someone looks out for you, empathizes with you, stands up for you, listens to you, relates to you, appreciates you, respects you, accepts you, or acknowledges you, they are giving you love!

When someone thanks you, encourages you, believes in you, supports you, forgives you, soothes you, uplifts you, or trusts you, they are giving you love!

When someone opens up to you, tries to know you, stays strong for you, assumes the best in you, compliments you, mentors you, makes time for you, or makes an effort for you, they are giving you love!

Love is always coming at us, in one form or another—sometimes from friends, sometimes from family, sometimes from strangers we may only know in passing. It might be a thoughtful call at just the right time, a spontaneous warm hug or an inspirational comment on a blog on a day when you felt weak and afraid. We all have so much love to give, and we're giving it every day. The only question is whether or not we are also able to recognize and really receive it.

I believe if you want to be loved, you need to love first. Reach out to others. Talk. Open up and reveal your feelings. Act lovingly. If someone you care about does not return your feelings, you can still act lovingly. You are responsible only for your own actions. This way there are no regrets. Giving unconditional love will bring peace, contentment and satisfaction to your life. It all begins with love!

DO THE PEOPLE IN YOUR LIFE KNOW HOW MUCH YOU LOVE THEM? If the answer is "no," then who do you need to talk to today to tell them how much you love them?

(17) A LOVE OF LEARNING
BE A STUDENT OF LIFE

A love of learning is the excitement, anticipation and curiosity of learning new skills, acquiring new knowledge or building on our existing skills and knowledge. A love of learning is an awareness of the endless flow of information that we are absorbing daily – minute by minute. A love of learning is the processing of that information and how it impacts or influences us, and ultimately, what we do with it.

A love of learning also encompasses the desire to take all of life's experiences, positive or negative, and learn from them. We need to see all life challenges as opportunities for us to learn and grow from rather than perceiving them as personal attacks. We need to look for the good and bad in all situations and understand what we can from these circumstances so we are better equipped to handle the next crises or challenge. We are the culmination of all of our life experiences and how we use those experiences is in direct correlation to the happiness and success we are seeking.

A love of learning is something we should practice as adults and absolutely instill in our children! It begins with role modeling and book knowledge and spills over into the areas of socialization and relationships. We typically want to protect our children and shield them from experiences that would probably make them stronger individuals in the end. Modeling a love of learning helps your child understand that when uncomfortable situations arise, they too, can actually learn from them. This philosophy will help carry them through childhood and into adulthood.

The benefits of loving to learn during the school years are obvious. Students who love to learn are more likely to engage in their schoolwork and receive positive feedback from teachers and parents. However, the benefits of this strength extend beyond the school years and into retirement. "Indeed, a love of learning may be particularly valuable during older age in that it may prevent cognitive decline. Research suggests that individuals who are able to develop and maintain interests later in life are likely to be more physically and mentally healthy than their less-engaged peers." (Krapp & Lewalter, 2001; Renninger & Shumar, 2002; Snowdon, 2001).

(E) *When I choose to use this tool, it allows me to look at each situation from the perspective that there is something for me to learn at that given moment. It forces me to be present focusing on what it is I'm supposed to be learning. I know that when I come from this perspective, I engage people in a way that they are clear that my focus and emotional availability is solely focused on them.*

(T) *A love of learning to me began with my first job in the insurance industry. My boss told me that I was going to be faced with lots of interesting challenges and experiences in this job and that I needed to learn something from each and every one of them. He said that in life I might face both good and bad challenges that come from both good and bad people. He added that it would be important to look at each personal experience and to file it away in my mental file cabinet under the heading of "good" and "bad." We will have a tendency to want to disregard the bad and only learn from the good things that happen. Learning from the bad things in life helps me avoid making mistakes that I've made before. All of my experiences make me who I am. The true value comes from what I've learned from those experiences.*

GAUGING YOUR LOVE OF LEARNING
Where do you measure up?

> **FAR LEFT (RED ZONE): YOU ARE FEARFUL OF LEARNING NEW THINGS OR TAKING ON NEW TASKS.**

- You choose to survive instead of thrive.
- You choose not to appreciate the wisdom you have already acquired through your own experiences.
- You choose to not ask for help or look for resources.

> **THE MIDDLE (GREEN ZONE): YOU LOVE LEARNING AND YOU ARE AN AVID STUDENT OF LIFE.**

- You are motivated to go from situation to situation, confident in your ability to assess what each situation has in store for you.
- You understand that you learn from each experience.
- You see your take-away lessons clearly.
- You are "in the moment—you are real."
- You are a student of life and all its lessons. You crave learning.
- You understand that being a student of life demands that you choose humility and sincerity.
- You see each situation as an opportunity not only to learn but to do better the next time. You seek opportunities for self-improvement.

> **FAR RIGHT (RED ZONE): YOU PRESENT YOURSELF AS A "KNOW-IT-ALL".**

- You act as if you have all the answers to cover the truth of feeling insecure.
- You present yourself as if you are excited about learning and that you are a student of life, while you really believe that you already have all the answers.
- You believe you won't be accepted if you don't have all the answers so you present yourself as a "know-it-all".
- You are not open to learning from others.

CONSIDER THIS!

 I walk the walk by applying these character tools. When counseling children and adolescents, I say, "I want to know what things look like through your eyes." At the end of a session, I ask them to tell me one thing they wish was a little different about our time together.

I say, "I ask you because I want to learn from you, too." This process falls under the heading of "A love of learning." The kids tell me they enjoy my asking them about themselves. They feel heard and understood by me wanting to know how things look to them. The kids feel valued. Children understand this concept even as young as four and five years of age. They can tell if I am "killing time" by my questions or if I really want to learn.

Are you genuinely interested in others, wanting to know more of their stories rather than telling your own? Are you aware of how you impact people when you show real interest in them? People are generally savvy, picking up on cues and are drawn to people who are interested in them.

My wife, Leslie says, "I feel that life is something that should be approached from the standpoint that we are always the student, moment to moment, from birth to death. Life always has a fresh restart. You will always be learning because there is always something new to learn."

TI am a student of life. I have to be in order to survive in my chosen profession. As such, I spend time being in the moment, where I have life clarity. When I am in the moment, I see the bigger picture of what I observe. I "get" more from what I hear and not much passes me by. This is how I live. I do not have to play "catch up," by counting on others to fill me in on what happened.

Everyone has a story to tell. Some are willing to tell that story with little prodding. Others are more private. But add to the mix an interested person with good listening skills and you have the beginning of a relationship. The driving force is the ability to engage people.

When you depend on others to fill you in, you get their perspective, not yours. I observe situations as they unfold. Why things happen and how people behave is of interest to me. I want to know how decisions affect the people making them – positively or negatively. People fascinate me. I pay rapt attention to my surroundings. Answers are found in seeing the details.

What are you choosing to focus on when connecting with people? Do you connect with the idea of having something to learn or do you place yourself in a teaching mode? Do you try to see yourself from another person's perspective, as if you were in that person's shoes?

I believe in the philosophy of Theodore Roosevelt who said, "People don't care how much you know but they do want to know how much you care." Every time I open a communication door with someone, business or personal, I am exuberant. The process brings me closer to becoming a better person, which feeds my passion for life.

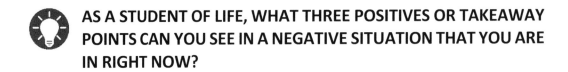 **AS A STUDENT OF LIFE, WHAT THREE POSITIVES OR TAKEAWAY POINTS CAN YOU SEE IN A NEGATIVE SITUATION THAT YOU ARE IN RIGHT NOW?**

 **HUMILITY**

The quality of humility is marked by modesty, peacefulness, quietness and an unassuming attitude. The opposite of humility is arrogance and pride. In today's culture, pride is celebrated and arrogance is almost a prerequisite to be taken seriously in business, politics and sports.

We often think that humility is only for wimps and losers. This is because we misunderstand the true meaning of humility. When we choose humility, we are placing the needs of our families, our work places and social circles above our own. This means that we are actively searching for opportunities to serve others and lift them up.

There is a difference between the strength in humility and the perceived strength in arrogance.

HUMILITY VS. ARROGANCE

- Humility learns; arrogance knows.
- Humility listens; arrogance talks.
- Humility serves others; arrogance serves ourselves.
- Humility builds others up. Arrogance builds ourselves up.
- Humility joins; arrogance stands aloof.
- Humility connects; arrogance disconnects.
- Humility enables us to ask, "How can I help?

 A statement I commonly make to people is, "Those who know, don't talk and those who talk, don't know." It is all about striking a healthy balance between humility and confidence. In other words, I have enough confidence in myself to lift others up without needing recognition for doing so.

My Peaceful Pete story: In my mid-twenties, I was a young gun regional marketing director responsible for teaching insurance agents to sell insurance. At the end of the year, they called all of us young corporate guys into a meeting to teach us to be better managers. In one segment of the meeting, they drew a line on the floor. At one end was a silhouette of a weak looking individual called "Peaceful Pete." At the other end of the line was a macho-looking individual called "Hardass Hank." Our class facilitator asked us all to choose where we fit on that line regarding our management techniques. As I was working with a number of young studs, there was a big fight to place themselves somewhere on that line between the middle and "Hardass Hank." Everyone thought that being a "Hardass Hank" was a better way of being a successful manager. In this process, I was pushed to the end of the line closest to "Peaceful Pete." I was humiliated. Everyone looked at me as weak in my management skills.

Now that I am 50-years-old and look back on my life of being a "Peaceful Pete," I realize that this is exactly where I was supposed to be. I see strength in humility and take joy in seeing and helping others succeed.

GAUGING YOUR SOCIAL AWARENESS
Where do you measure up?

> **FAR LEFT (RED ZONE): YOU DON'T EXERCISE HUMILITY IN YOUR DAILY LIFE.**

- You are arrogant.
- You are a braggart.
- You are not interested in serving others.

- You do not brag.
- You understand that you are not the center of the universe.
- You do not regard yourself as superior to others.
- You let your accomplishments speak for themselves.
- You refuse to "one-up" others in relationships.
- You avoid flaunting or seeking to be the center of attention.
- You take joy in lifting others up and seeing them succeed.

- You use the appearance of humility with the intention of manipulating others.
- You use the appearance of humility for self-serving purposes.
- You use humility at the cost of others.
- You confuse humility by presenting yourself as passive or having low esteem.

CONSIDER THIS!

 You can better understand and apply humility by looking at humility in these three different ways. You understand that the universe is larger than just meeting your individual wants and needs. Humility is your ability to serve others with no strings attached. Serving others makes you a stronger person. Humility is the outcome when you recognize and acknowledge that you cannot do it on your own. It's the point when you connect with God. You invite God into your life because you realize you cannot do it on your own.

When you choose to use humility, it gives you a whole different vantage point from which to view your world. Humility allows you to sit back and take in everything that is going on in a conversation or situation without feeling the need to say something. It allows you to assess all the different needs and characteristics of the situation that is going on and look for the proper entry point to help and lift people up. It truly allows you to see things for the way they really are.

TODAY, I CAN PRACTICE HUMILITY IN MY RELATIONSHIPS WITH THE PEOPLE IN MY LIFE BY.....

RESILIENCY

Resiliency is the ability to recover from stress and adversity. Resilient people are flexible, positive and project a degree of confidence. Resiliency allows us to get through daily stress and life challenges. Resilient people are able to recover from difficult situations without lasting effects and difficulties. In fact, the more resilient you are, the more quickly you are able to recover from situations that would pull the rug out from under those with little resiliency.

In today's culture, there is a tendency to blame others for our miseries and suffering. We assume the victim role with this mind-set, which is the exact opposite of resiliency. When we are in a victim role, our focus is on blaming others for where we are or how we feel in a given moment. We do not take any responsibility or accountability. Therefore, we feel we have no choice or control in the outcome. At this point, we are waiting for somebody to say or do something to resolve our struggle because we cannot do it ourselves. "I need to wait for you to apologize or make amends with me before I can move forward." As a consequence, it takes away our initiative to be resilient and create the outcome we desire.

When we choose resiliency, we have the ability to experience negative and positive situations and find redeeming qualities and opportunities in both. We look at the challenges we face as opportunities for us to grow as individuals. We find it is better to move toward the pain searching for opportunities to learn instead of running or hiding from it. This is where you believe that adversity should be dealt with head-on and see the value of choosing resiliency. Resilience is the process of adapting to difficult or challenging life experiences, says the late Al Siebert, PhD, founder of The Resiliency Center in Portland, Oregon. Curious to know how your own resilience rates? Take this quiz, adapted from Siebert's book.

The Resiliency Advantage.

Rate yourself from 1-5 (1 = strongly disagree 5 = strongly agree):

1) I'm usually optimistic. I see difficulties as temporary and expect to overcome them.
2) Feelings of anger, loss and discouragement don't last long.
3) I can tolerate high levels of ambiguity and uncertainty about situations.
4) I adapt quickly to new developments. I'm curious. I ask questions.
5) I'm playful. I find the humor in rough situations, and can laugh at myself.
6) I learn valuable lessons from my experiences and from the experiences of others.
7) I'm good at solving problems. I'm good at making things work well.
8) I'm strong and durable. I hold up well during tough times.
9) I've converted misfortune into good luck and found benefits in bad experiences.

Less than 20: Low Resilience — You may have trouble handling pressure or setbacks, and may feel deeply hurt by any criticism. When things don't go well, you may feel helpless and without hope. Consider seeking some professional counsel or support in developing your resiliency skills. Connect with others who share your developmental goals.

20–30: Some Resilience — You have some valuable pro-resiliency skills, but also plenty of room for improvement. Strive to strengthen the characteristics you already have and to cultivate the characteristics you lack. You may also wish to seek some outside coaching or support.

30–35: Adequate Resilience — You are a self-motivated learner who recovers well from most challenges. Learning more about resilience, and consciously building your resiliency skills, will empower you to find more joy in life, even in the face of adversity.

35–45: Highly Resilient — You bounce back well from life's setbacks and can thrive even under pressure. You could be of service to others who are trying to cope better with adversity.

E *When I choose the quality of resiliency, I am reminding myself to be focused on the present and what is in front of me that I can change rather than continuing to focus on aspects that I cannot change. When I choose resiliency, I am consciously choosing to move forward.*

T *I feel I am a resilient person who has learned to rely on my ability to recover from stressful happenings. Without resiliency, I would not be able to live up to my daily responsibilities and take care of those who count on me. I feel that being resilient is the key to success. To be resilient requires a degree of courage as well. It is what allows me to "step back into the batter box" after being hit, so to speak. Being in sales has required a degree of resiliency as an emotional safety net. I know that every "no" means I'm that much closer to a "yes."*

GAUGING YOUR RESILIENCY
Where do you measure up?

FAR LEFT (RED ZONE): YOU CHOOSE TO HAVE A VICTIM MENTALITY.

- You choose to not recover from stress or life crises.
- You choose to not forgive or accept the past.
- You choose to focus on injustice and revenge.
- You choose to not take risks.

> **THE MIDDLE (GREEN ZONE): YOU SEE OPPORTUNITIES TO LEARN AND MOVE FORWARD REGARDLESS OF WHAT IS HAPPENING.**

- You learn from mistakes instead of denying they ever happened.
- You see obstacles as challenges you can navigate around.
- You use adversity and obstacles as a means to make you stronger.
- You face challenges head-on rather than seeing yourself as helpless and powerless – a victim of those challenges.

> **FAR RIGHT (RED ZONE): YOU CHOOSE RESILIENCY AT THE EXPENSE OF OTHERS.**

- You choose to move forward without taking your family's needs or emotions into consideration.
- You say to yourself, "I'm going to do what I want at all costs".
- Your forward movement does not honor or value the magnitude of the situation.
- You plow ahead without paying attention to what needs to be dealt with or learned.

CONSIDER THIS!

 When you choose to be resilient, you are choosing to be connected to your spiritual self. When spirituality is part of your being, you are not just going through the motions of life. You believe in the bigger picture where everything you experience in your life is moving you towards something greater.

 Resiliency is another one of those little secrets of success in life. Being resilient allows you to keep plodding, putting one foot in front of the other even when you don't want to and feel there is no way you can go forward. Going forward through life's challenges with resiliency makes you strong and confident that no matter what happens, everything will be okay. Going through life knowing everything will be okay will give you the peace, contentment and satisfaction that you are looking for.

IF I WERE MORE RESILIENT IN MY LIFE, I WOULD.....

 **INTEGRITY**

Integrity can be defined as an adherence to a code of moral values, principles and character tools. Integrity speaks to demonstrating a consistency in your actions that are in alignment with your personal values and principles.

Integrity is speaking the truth and presenting oneself in a genuine way. Integrity is being open and honest about your own thoughts, emotions and responsibilities. Integrity is being very careful to not mislead others through your actions or your failure to act. Integrity is presenting yourself as the same person regardless of who is in front of you. Integrity can be summed up simply as doing the right thing for the right reason even when no one is watching.

THE INTEGRITY METER

Consider this tool as an integrity meter or a gauge which indicates your level of integrity. This integrity meter is similar to a voltage meter that all good carpenters keep in their tool box. The voltage meter is important to the carpenter because it helps him/her make sure that the power flowing through the house has the correct voltage. When your home has the correct voltage running through it, everything works at its optimum performance.

This voltage meter is analogous to your integrity meter because the more character tools that you integrate into your life, the higher your integrity meter rates. The higher your integrity meter rates, the more you are operating at your optimum performance. For you to operate at optimum performance, you must strive to be in the green zone of every tool that you use. The more character tools that you utilize in the green zone every day, the more peace, contentment and satisfaction you will have in your daily life.

I believe that integrity is the integration of all our character tools into our daily lives. It is my experience as a therapist that the integrity of families, marriages and all the encompassing relationships is driven by the degree of the integrity of each person. When everyone exercises a high degree of integrity, relationships are at their strongest and healthiest.

*I believe that integrity is a culmination of all the tools in the **Timeless Twenty Toolkit©**. It is imperative for us to strive to use as many of these tools in our daily lives as possible. I believe that when you add integrity to a sincere desire to lift up those around you, you will experience the happiness you are looking for. Integrity simply means that you are looking at all the responsibilities in your life and living up to them the best you possibly can.*

GAUGING YOUR INTEGRITY
Where do you measure up?

> **FAR LEFT (RED ZONE): YOU ARE DISHONEST AND CHOOSE NOT TO USE CHARACTER TOOLS.**

- You are dishonest.
- You are untrustworthy-your words and behaviors do not match.
- You are inconsistent and unpredictable.
- You are unethical.

> **THE MIDDLE (GREEN ZONE): YOU ARE UTILIZING ALL YOUR CHARACTER TOOLS IN THE GREEN ZONE.**

- You are the same person no matter who is looking.
- You make healthy choices even when you don't think someone is watching you.
- You are trustworthy.
- People learn they can rely on you.
- Your choices support your values and goals so that you are not sabotaging your better self.

- Your words and actions are at the cost of someone else.
- You are 100% bluntly honest without utilizing empathy and sensitivity.

CONSIDER THIS!

 Your integrity is your golden egg. Choosing to use each of these character strengths when no one is looking and when you know you won't get any credit for it is when you are at your strongest. The more character tools you choose to use, the higher level of integrity you have and the stronger you are as a person.

 As the rebar is the strength of your home's foundation, character tools are the strength of your personal foundation. The strength of your personal foundation is called integrity. The more integrity you have, the stronger your foundation. The stronger your foundation, the stronger your relationships. The stronger your relationships, the more peace, contentment and satisfaction you will experience in life.

 THREE AREAS IN MY LIFE THAT WOULD BENEFIT FROM ME CHOOSING INTEGRITY ARE.....

USE YOUR TOOLKIT
TO REACH YOUR CABIN

**We have given you a set of reliable tools to help move you toward
your cabin in a healthy manner despite whatever
emotion you are feeling.**

*Let's say, for a moment, that one of my cabins is to have a healthy relationship with
my wife. Does that mean that I must use all of the character tools, all of the time, every
time? No, but when I focus on using one character tool and using it well, it is like the
domino effect. The other character strengths naturally follow.*

*When I build my cabin with Leslie, my first step is to grab the character tool "Hope and
Optimism" from my toolbox. This tool reminds me that things are going to work out
and that all of our experiences move us towards something greater.*

 *Next, I consider which tool will further enhance my relationship with my wife.
Choosing the character tool "Relationship Awareness" helps me pay more
attention to her needs. I'd be more aware of when she is struggling or
whether or not she is happy.*

*Then, I add the tool "Humor and Playfulness" as a reminder to not take things too
seriously!*

*Finally, I add the tool "Gratitude" to complete my cabin. Gratitude allows me to focus
on what I **do** have with my wife, versus what I **do not** have. I have become very aware
that my cabin with my wife, Leslie, is only as strong as the foundation we've built. A
foundation that is built with character tools offers stability, consistency and
predictability. It has been my absolute experience that using these character tools has
helped me create the strongest relationship possible with Leslie. Our relationship is
solid because we have a foundation built with these character tools.*

*These tools are user friendly and always accessible to you. The best way to remember the tools is to **be** them. For example, if you need more courage in your life, then you need to see yourself as a courageous person. If you want to be more honest, you need to see yourself as an honest person. If you want to forgive, you need to see yourself as a forgiving person.*

Can you see how using all these tools contributes to a healthy relationship? Your specific cabin represents its own special relationship requiring an individualized selection of tools. It is up to you to choose the tools that most apply to each of your cabins.

This intense process requires focus and commitment. Imagine your character tools as muscles. The more you choose to use them, the stronger you become! Initially you may feel clumsy and awkward handling these tools. However, the more consistently you use that "character muscle", the easier it becomes to choose that character strength to reach your desired cabin.

No self-help book meets every need for every person. A skilled counselor can assist you if you find yourself stuck in any of these areas. We do believe that the exercise of these strengths will contribute to a life of peace, contentment and satisfaction for you and those around you.

We designed this book to be a blue print to your happiness – a detailed and reliable plan to your success!

A NEW BEGINNING
Shall WE Dance?

YES! RELATIONSHIPS ARE LIKE DANCES!

Troy and Jeni learned from their dance lessons how to reconnect and rebuild their relationship from the ground up. They learned how to communicate and respond to each other. It made them stronger as a couple and gave them a "home base" to return to if they made a "misstep."

The dance lessons increased their ability to work together. Troy and Jeni were able to compromise more and be more forgiving with each other. They learned there are similarities between the steps taken in a dance to make it a good dance, and the steps to be taken in a relationship to make it a good relationship.

When the dance is in sync and the relationship is healthy, a couple will move with each other providing a frame of trust, support and connection. This is how to cultivate a relationship with one another on and off the dance floor.

When you liken all your relationships to the dance, you see yourself as having an active role in that relationship. If you don't see yourself as dancing with each person in a relationship, you won't see yourself as getting involved with them. If you can't see yourself getting involved with them, how in the world can you get a rewarding experience from that relationship?

YOUR SAVINGS ACCOUNTS

Look at each of your relationships as if each is a savings account. Are you making enough deposits to cover the withdrawals? In other words, are you putting enough emotional "deposits" into your relationships so that your relationship "accounts" are not depleted? Just as with a bank account, when withdrawals outnumber deposits, the account will be overdrawn. On the other hand, when you keep deposits coming, you'll have an active account that will not be depleted. The same theory can be applied to relationships. It is far better to put more into relationships than to keep withdrawing until they are depleted.

Be aware of your actions and be consistent in keeping those deposits coming. If you want to guarantee that your relationships are solid, make sure that your deposits always outweigh your withdrawals.

E *I often notice that when "deposits" are made in a relationship, the deposit is self-serving. For example, I might think of buying my wife, Leslie, some chocolate. Nice thought, yes? It would be except I am the one who loves chocolate! Get the idea? The gesture might feel good but the gift only benefits me.*

Think of a "deposit" as something that is intended to lift up the other person. In this case, I might instead give Leslie an extra hug and a kiss upon greeting her. I know that my "deposit" will be received as it was intended and I know I am sending Leslie the message of "I love you and I want to lift you up."

T *What does a deposit look like? A deposit is a behavior or words that would be a symbol or a sign of your love and investment in the relationship. Your deposits need to be genuine and with the other person's best interests in mind. Deposits can include understanding the other individual, attending to the "little things" and keeping commitments. Deposits should be made often and throughout the day and with consistency.*

Likewise, what does a withdrawal look like? A withdrawal happens any time we have a disagreement or say something hurtful. A withdrawal is when someone misinterprets what is said or any time we get off track with one another. A healthy relationship is when our deposits clearly outweigh the withdrawals.

☀ "THE TIMELESS TWENTY TOOLKIT©"

Put your focus on the character tools we have presented and apply them to your relationships and situations around you. These tools are simple and user friendly.

The Timeless Twenty Toolkit© is designed to help you make healthy choices that will strengthen your relationships. We encourage you to focus on how you respond to the people and situations you encounter throughout your day. Remember…shoot for the green zone!

E *Fear is the only emotion that will stop us from choosing to use the character tools. For example, focusing on fear or its resulting anger will stop us from choosing to use the character tool, **honesty** – if we let it. "I am afraid that if I am honest, I will be rejected."*

*Focusing on fear will stop us from choosing to use the character tool, **forgiveness** – if we let it. The fear is that it might communicate the message that what is being forgiven is okay. "If I forgive you, you might think that it is okay to do what you did to me or that you can continue to do what you are doing to me."*

*Focusing on fear will stop us from choosing to use the character tool, **courage** –if we let it. "I do not have the courage to be vulnerable and connect with other people because I am afraid I will be hurt again."*

It is profoundly important that we understand that we do have the choice to be motivated either by our thoughts and emotions (focusing on "me") or be motivated by our character strengths (focusing on others). Our thoughts and emotions keep us focused on ourselves. The character strengths keep us focused on the people and the relationships in our life.

T *We have a tendency to focus on things that have happened in the past that have brought us pain and suffering or to focus on the future that is full of fear and anxiety. We know it is important to focus and stay in the present but we don't know how. **The Timeless Twenty Toolkit©** can only be used in the present. The tools force you to get outside of yourself and focus on the situation or relationship that is in front of you.*

We invite you to dance with us! It is our heartfelt and sincere intention to inspire you to see yourself as an equal partner with the variety of people who cross your path. We want the concept of the **Timeless Twenty Toolkit**© to ripple through your life and create change! We live these tools and want you to feel that same passion as well!

We want to support you through the process of using these tools in your daily life. We want to dance with you so that we become a community of help and support for each other.

Join us at www.erikandtroy.com

Shall We Dance? A Guide to Happiness is just the beginning! Our intent is to stay connected with you through our website, social media blog, podcast, workshops and seminars. We invite you to stay in touch with us. Tell us how the *Timeless Twenty Toolkit*© has influenced your relationships, your life and your dances! Share your newfound power and success, as well as your challenges so others can learn from you.

FRIENDS HELPING FRIENDS.

LET'S HAVE EACH OTHER'S BACKS!

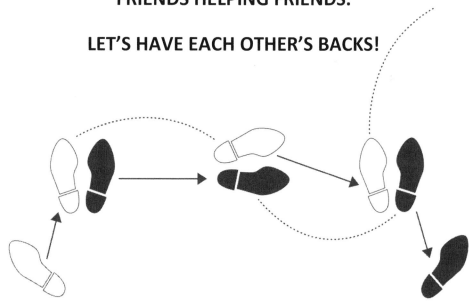

ERIK&TROY

Like us on Facebook!

www.erikandtroy.com

Made in the USA
San Bernardino, CA
04 August 2014